GROWING UP IN A LAND CALLED EGYPT

Shawnee Books

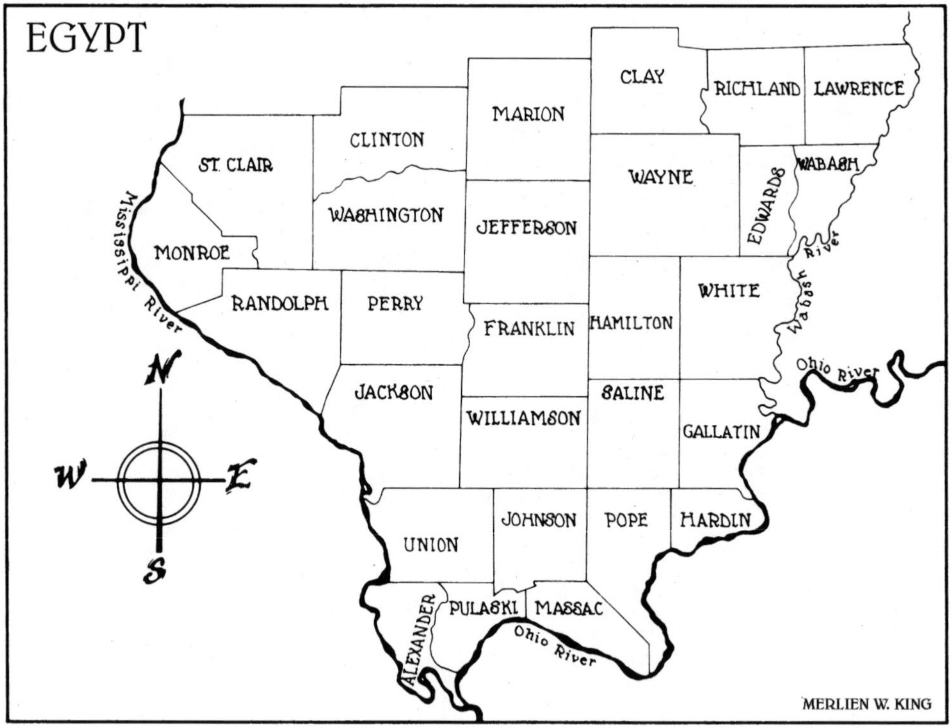
EGYPT
ST. CLAIR
CLINTON
MARION
CLAY
RICHLAND
LAWRENCE
WAYNE
EDWARDS
WABASH
MONROE
WASHINGTON
JEFFERSON
RANDOLPH
PERRY
FRANKLIN
HAMILTON
WHITE
JACKSON
WILLIAMSON
SALINE
GALLATIN
UNION
JOHNSON
POPE
HARDIN
ALEXANDER
PULASKI
MASSAC
Mississippi River
Wabash River
Ohio River
Ohio River
N
S
E
W
MERLIEN W. KING

Growing Up in a Land Called Egypt

A SOUTHERN ILLINOIS FAMILY BIOGRAPHY

CLEO CARAWAY

With a Foreword by Ben Gelman

Southern Illinois University Press / *Carbondale*

Printed in the United States of America

23 22 21 20 5 4 3 2

Cover illustration: a gathering of the Caraway clan at the home place during World War II

Library of Congress Cataloging-in-Publication Data
Caraway, Cleo.
Growing up in a land called Egypt : a southern Illinois family biography / Cleo Caraway ; with a foreword by Ben Gelman.
p. cm. — (Shawnee books)
ISBN-13: 978-0-8093-2946-5 (pbk. : alk. paper)
ISBN-10: 0-8093-2946-8 (pbk. : alk. paper)
1. Caraway, Cleo—Childhood and youth—Anecdotes. 2. Murphysboro Region (Ill.)—Social life and customs—20th century—Anecdotes. 3. Depressions—1929—Illinois—Murphysboro Region—Anecdotes. 4. Country life—Illinois—Murphysboro Region—Anecdotes. 5. Caraway family—Anecdotes. I. Title.
F549.M98C37 2010
977.3′994—dc22
[B] 2009021332

Printed on recycled paper ♲

To the pioneer mother, of southern Illinois and of regions near and far, who moved heaven and earth to rear her children in hard times and in such a way that one day they would "arise up, and call her blessed" (Proverbs 31:28, The Holy Bible, KJV)

In Memoriam

> Bessie Mae Rowan Caraway (1892–1963)
> The wound of her passing will not heal . . .
> But the cool shadows and dazzling brights of her memory
> Are like leaf-filtered sunshine strewn across the void.

Johanna Kelley Rowan, we never knew you. A daughter of immigrants from the Emerald Isle, you died at twenty-eight, two days after the death of your infant Lucy. I remember the trips we made to your gravesite in the Rowan Cemetery at Makanda. Mother wanted your grave to look nice and brought bouquets of velvet roses to place there. I recall her palpable sorrow as we worked around your headstone. She was only nine years old when you left her May 18, 1901, but she remembered you well.

If you could have known your surviving daughter Bessie Mae as an adult, you would have been so proud. She grew up to be a beautiful woman, with curly auburn hair, sky blue eyes, and a peaches-and-cream complexion. She married a handsome young man named Charless Caraway as she approached her eighteenth birthday. Even on the occasion of her fiftieth wedding anniversary celebration—after a lifetime of hard work, seven children, and the onset of a fatal illness—she was easily the most arresting woman there. But it wasn't her physical attributes alone that distinguished her. Bessie was a lady with erect carriage, a certain tilt of her head, a gracious demeanor, and a spark in the eye. She was imbued with an indomitable spirit, with a genuine zest for life and living. She was courageous and strong and ardently devoted to her family. And time could not diminish these qualities.

So rest easy in your tomb with your wee bonnie babe, Johanna. The green grass grows all around. We will never forget you. You were our mother's mother.

Contents

Illustrations

Foreword

Ben Gelman

Cleo Caraway's fond recollections of her life as a young girl during the Great Depression in southern Illinois are more than a sugary dose of nostalgia. In preparing to write *Growing Up in a Land Called Egypt: A Southern Illinois Family Biography*, she backed up her personal reminiscences with some solid research.

When Cleo recalls that there was a "copy machine" in the library of the one-room schoolhouse where she learned her three R's, she explains that it was a "hectograph," which made use of ink implants transferred to a tray of gelatin from which copies could be made as needed.

And when she writes about shopping with her mother at Ross's Store in Murphysboro, for example, she provides not only a photograph of the store on Walnut Street but also a capsule biography of owner Sam Ross, who remained active in business into his eighties and lived to be ninety-six.

There's a solid, fleshed-out quality to the stories Cleo tells of her experiences as one of seven children on a Jackson County farm in the late 1920s and the 1930s—going to school and to church and making do with far less than children expect today and yet living a full life.

Part of the three-dimensional aspect of the book can be attributed to the fact that it tells, from another viewpoint, stories related by the author's father,

Charless Caraway, in his book, *Foothold on a Hillside: Memories of a Southern Illinoisan* (Southern Illinois University Press), about how he carved out a life for himself and his family on a southern Illinois hill farm. But it is not necessary to read her father's book before reading this one. Cleo Caraway's work stands on its own. And her loving references to her father's writings lend a special quality to this book.

There is a wonderful feeling of family, not just in the stories about her father and mother, sisters and brothers, grandparents and cousins, but in the ones about good neighbors and friends. They are the kind of stories all of us would like to remember about our own families.

Finally, a word about the illustrations in this book. Cleo went not only to her own and her friends' photo albums but also to historical sources to show us the many real-life characters that people this book and the places where they lived their lives. Especially noteworthy are the captions. Unlike the terse, unsatisfactory notes often found beneath the pictures in this kind of book, they provide a wealth of detailed information that complements the text.

This is more than just one woman's account of growing up at a certain time in a particular corner of America. It touches something in all of us that cherishes the best of our treasured childhood memories.

GROWING UP IN A LAND CALLED EGYPT

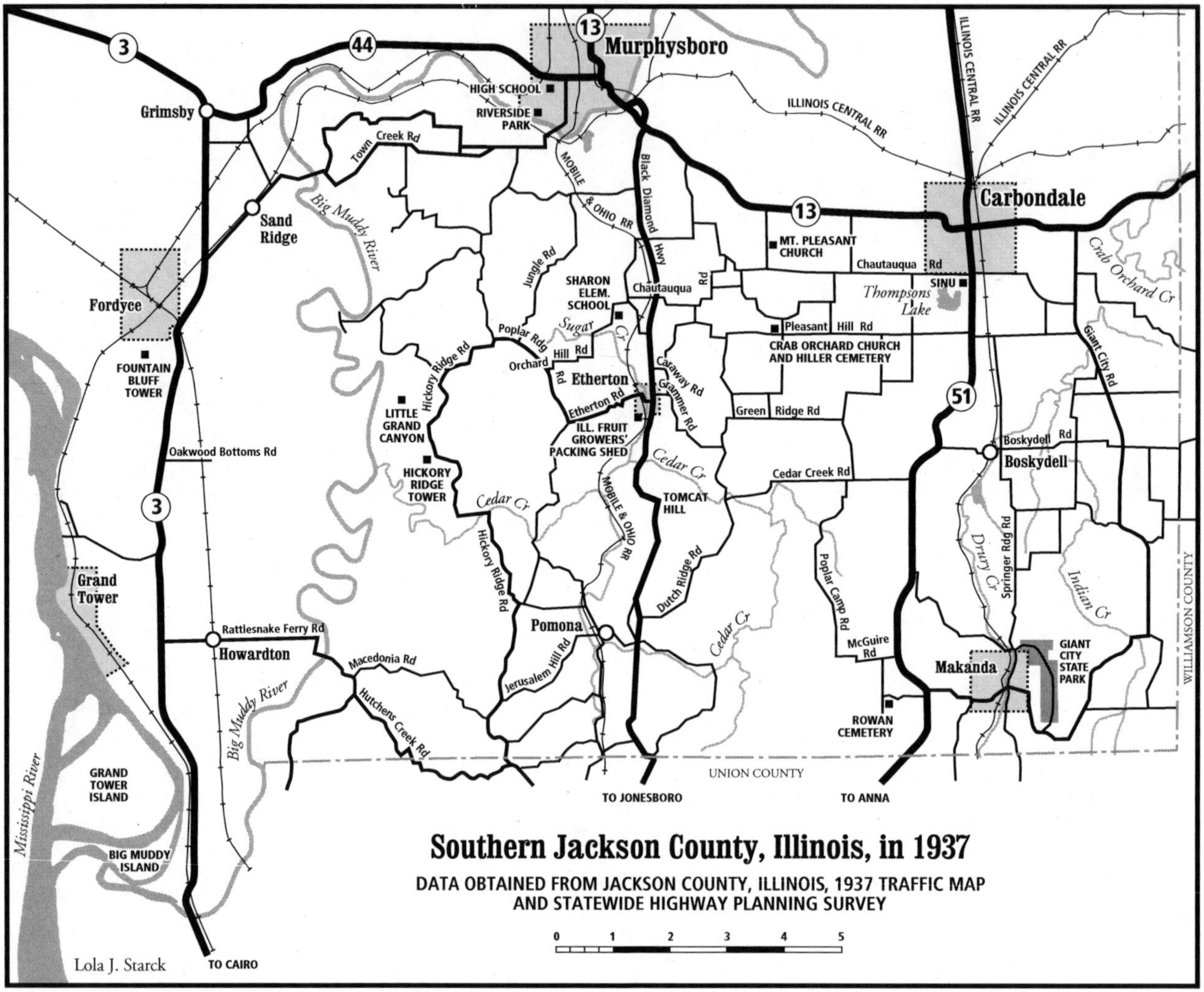

The area south of Murphysboro and Carbondale in the 1930s, with some of the locations mentioned in the text of this book. Some names have not survived to the present day: route 44 is now route 149, for instance, and the Black Diamond Highway, named for the coal mines in the area, is now route 127. Caraway Road, labeled here (*near the center of the map*) to show where the Caraways lived, was not given that name officially until the 1970s. The names of other secondary roads shown here were in common usage in the time frame of this book and are now official road names. The Mobile & Ohio Railroad (*upper and lower center of the map*) underwent several changes before affiliating with the Illinois Central Railroad, now part of the Canadian National Railroad.

Introduction

One southern Illinois legend has it that settlers in the northern part of the state, like the biblical Jacob and his sons, "came down into Egypt" to buy grain when their own crops failed the summer of 1831. Another holds that southern Illinois was called Egypt and many of its towns were named for ancient Egyptian forerunners because the delta formed by the confluence of the Ohio and Mississippi rivers resembles the Nile delta in Africa's Egypt. Both legends, rooted in area history of the early 1800s, seem to account for a continuing fascination with our intriguing links with the Old World.

While delving into source material, I found a natural bridge between the southern Illinois legends and my own reminiscences on the conspiracy of fate that brought my ancestors from two distant and antagonistic lands—England in the 1600s and Ireland in the 1800s—so that my father and mother would be married in a southern Illinois village in 1910.

In *Foothold on a Hillside: Memories of a Southern Illinoisan* (Southern Illinois University Press, 1986), my father, Charless Caraway, related the story of how he and his bride, Bessie Mae Rowan, met and married in Makanda, Illinois, and then struggled to establish for themselves and their children a foothold in southern Illinois. He proudly tells of the births of their first two sons, Lester and George, when they were living in Makanda Township. Of son Wayne and daughter Ethel after their move to Murphysboro Township. And of daughter Cleo, son Charley, and daughter Betty at the home place near Etherton Switch.

With *Foothold* as a backdrop for my own recollections, images wedged in a time slot between the market crash of 1929 and the early World War II years literally tumbled from my memory onto the written page. And often, as you will soon see, these same images sent me to the libraries to search eagerly for their reflections from the past.

Growing Up in a Land Called Egypt: A Southern Illinois Family Biography records the coming of age of the Caraway children on the family farm. Highlighted along the way are the memorable people, places, and events we encountered in a land called Egypt . . . and beyond. I hope that my vivid recollections will be "like apples of gold in pictures of silver" (from Proverbs 25:11, The Holy Bible, KJV) for my readers.

Part One ❧ Childhood Days

'How dear to this heart are the scenes of my childhood,
When fond recollection recalls them to view,
The orchard, the meadow, the deep-tangled wildwood,
And every loved spot which my infancy knew.
—Samuel Woodworth, "The Old Oaken Bucket"

With a Song in Our Hearts

With absolute clarity, I remember the day my mother let me go to Sharon School with my older brother and sister, Wayne and Ethel, for the first time. I stood impatiently in the well-worn path that cut diagonally across our front yard and wound down the steep embankment to the roadbed as my mother issued unnecessary instructions concerning me. I could handle it!

That landmark day was sometime in the spring of 1930. I had turned five in March and would enter the first grade at Sharon late that summer. My mother wanted to prepare me for the big event. She needn't have worried. I was to have an enviable beginning.

Lena Doody, Mary Louise Harold, Farrell McClelland, Gertrude Cannon, and Mae Allen would be my grade school teachers. Mrs. Doody proved to be an ideal teacher and an interesting person, besides. She lived just a few yards down the road from the school, in a big white house with a handsome man, her husband, Fred. They met in 1907 at the Jamestown Tercentennial Exposition at Hampton Roads, Virginia (the three-hundredth anniversary of the first permanent English settlement in America), and corresponded for a year or so while Fred completed his military duty in the United States and the Philippines and Lena continued her teaching career. They were married just a few days after Fred returned to southern Illinois and then left to set up housekeeping in

The November 8, 1908, wedding portrait of Fred R. (age twenty-five) and Lena Waller Doody (age nineteen).

Caribou, Maine, Fred's hometown, with the promise that they would return if Lena didn't like living in the East.

I remember the first time I heard Mrs. Doody play the piano for our morning exercises. With the flag up, the bell rung, and the students assembled, we stood, hands over hearts, and recited the Pledge of Allegiance. A rousing rendition of "Yankee Doodle" followed, with the students high-stepping all around the classroom.

After the wake-up exercises, we stood tall at our desks and sang soulfully,

"My Bonnie lies over the ocean,
My Bonnie lies over the sea,
My Bonnie lies over the ocean,
Oh, bring back my Bonnie to me."

And

"Oh my darling, oh my darling,
Oh my darling Clementine!
You are lost and gone forever,
Dreadful sorry, Clementine."

Then we concluded with a spirited

"Frère Jacques, Frère Jacques,
Dormez vous, Dormez vous?
Sonnez les matines,
Sonnez les matines,
Din, dan, don; din, dan, don."

And

The Doody family (Fred, Lena, and baby son, Ashton) in 1911, at their home just a few yards down the road from Sharon School. After a one-year stay in Caribou, Maine, where Ashton was born, the family returned to southern Illinois and bought this home and the surrounding sixty acres of land. They sold the home in 1938 and moved to Murphysboro. Fred, of Irish ancestry, died in 1975 at ninety-one years of age, and Lena, of English descent, died in 1983 at ninety-three.

"Alouette, jentille alouette,
Alouette, je te plumerai."

These strange new words were enunciated carefully for the new students, and we were singing along in a more or less accurate fashion before the session was over.

Morning exercises were just a taste of what would come. On Friday afternoons, classes were abbreviated so we could work in a full hour of entertainment. My heart swelled when we sang

"By thy rivers gently flowing,
Illinois, Illinois, . . ."

Or

"My country, 'tis of thee,
Sweet land of liberty,
Of thee I sing . . ."
Then came a round like
"Row, row, row your boat
Gently down the stream,
Merrily, merrily, merrily, merrily,
Life is but a dream."

Occasionally, Roberta Moore, Ethel's classmate and friend, would, with a little coaxing, sing, "When the Red, Red Robin Comes Bob Bob Bobbin Along" and "Redwing."

Thus Mrs. Doody primed us for the experience of learning with an oil of gladness called song. No matter that some of us could not carry a tune. We learned in those little impromptu musicales that the heart can sing.

Over the Brook and Thro' the Wood

Sharon Elementary was a one-room school, if you didn't count the added space. Two cloakrooms had shelves for dinner buckets and hooks for coats and individual tin cups. We pumped our drinking water from a well in the school yard. The bellpull hung in the entrance hall. And there was an enchanting little library. In the schoolroom itself, desks of various sizes were arranged in rows on the bare, wooden floors. The blackboard, one of the teacher's prime tools of learning and punishment, ran the breadth of the front wall just beneath a pendulum clock and Stuart's portrait of George Washington. The teacher's desk sat squarely front and center. The left corner of the room was occupied by an upright piano, and a long recitation bench sat at the right. A large, coal-fired furnace, with a metal jacket to protect the careless or curious student, stood at the rear. Two more benches for visiting parents or guests sat against the back wall. This was the world in which about thirty youngsters from the surrounding farming community and a teacher lived from nine A.M. to three P.M. on weekdays. Once we were there, the options were nil.

Our trek to school, however, was another story. If we kept to our country lane, Route 127 north, and secondary roads to the west, the walk was about three miles. I learned that there was a much more fascinating way to get there. Mr. Ross's barbed wire–enclosed pasture was the forbidden route. Alice should have had such a wonderland. There were hills to climb and race down, great trees to hide behind, a stream with a rocky bed to ford, a great gully to hurdle, green glades in which to linger, and much more.

The children of half a dozen or more families—the numbers increased as we went along—set out on these daily excursions with all the ardor of a real expedition.

The pasture was off-limits, of course, because it contained a herd of cattle, including an ever-present bull. Our headlong flights through the fence to avoid being trampled or gored produced an interesting assortment of three-cornered tears in jackets, pants, shirts, dresses, and even underwear and socks.

Sharon School on inspection day, September 25, 1929. Note the pump at the right and the dirt road to the left, which took the author and her classmates past the Doody and Ross homes. This school was built in 1915, when the old Sharon School, on the George Golliher place about a quarter of a mile from this location, burned. Pictured here are members of the student body the year the author visited the school before enrolling the following fall. *First row (seated left to right)*: Carl Raines, Charles King, Jack Raines, John Morefield, Jesse Morefield, and Wayne Caraway. *Second row*: unidentified, Ethel Caraway, Roberta Moore, Alma Waller, Janetta Woodside, and Bernice Woodside. *Third row*: Norman Woodside, Charles Morefield, Esther Morefield, Dorothy Woodside, Lillian Ross, and Catherine Raines. In the rear are Lewis "Eb" Etherton, the Jackson County superintendent of schools, and Mrs. Lena Doody, the teacher.

But the secrets in that wooded pastureland called us. On a warm spring day, the meadows of wildflowers were somehow more inviting than our own and could keep us for hours past the appointed arrival time at home. In-season wild grapes begged to be sampled and caused a variety of finger, face, and clothing stains, not to mention stomachaches.

On snowy days, when the hills and dales could surprise us with drifts too deep for little folk to navigate, older brothers went along and carried us piggyback over the danger zones. The altitude of some of those rides seemed more precarious than the drifts!

A railroad track just outside the pasture fence greeted us in the morning and urged us out of the woods in the afternoon with the promise of a loud toot, a friendly wave from the engineer of the oncoming train, and boxcars to count until we were dizzy with the challenge.

As we neared the school in the mornings or left it in the afternoons, we picked up or dropped off five of the Milton children who lived on the Woods place and the two Perrigan children who lived in the log house by the railroad tracks on another farm that adjoined Mr. Ross's land. Mr. Perrigan, who worked on the farm, built the small cabin for himself and his son and daughter, Eugene and Leona. I thought their cabin in the wooded dell unutterably charming, and I still find myself longing to take one more stroll past the place where it once stood and through the pasture as we did all those years ago.

As I prepared to record images and impressions of this idyllic time in our young lives, I searched my own memories and asked schoolmates for their recollections. We all remembered fondly how the bell at Sharon School called us to our studies from the outdoor wonderlands where we tarried. But a nostalgic note from Roberta Moore Parmley brought to mind that on a clear day when the wind was right, we could also hear the bells from Rock Hill and Poplar Ridge Schools, the cowbells from neighboring pastures, and even the dinner bells from surrounding farms. The sounds fell softly on the ear then and echo still.

A country manse that the author and her brothers, sisters, and schoolmates passed on their way to and from school, when they chose to walk the roads instead of cutting through the pasture. Pictured here are William J. and Mary E. Waller with their children (*left to right*: Edgar, Joe, Lena, and Ethel) in 1898. Lena married Fred Doody in a ceremony in the bay window at the left of the photo. The Wallers sold the place to Charles Ross in 1919. Charles and Anna Schneider Ross, both descendants of German immigrants who came to America in the mid-1800s, were the parents of six children: Delia, Anna, Arthur, Eleanor, Carl, and Lillian. The Ross family sold their home place in 1947.

Readin' and 'Ritin' and 'Rithmetic

God wove a web of loveliness
Of clouds and stars and birds,
But made not any thing at all
So beautiful as words.
—Anna H. Branch, "Her Words"

Four young Miltons, after the family moved from the Woods place near Sharon School to the Bierer fruit farm (later known as Springdale Orchards) in 1937. Marion Milton (born March 30, 1880, in Princeton, Kentucky) had four children—Otho, Mary, Lloyd, and Robert—by his first wife, Eliza Ann Lott Milton, who died in 1911. In 1916 he married Florence Horsford (born September 8, 1896, in Fort Henry, Tennessee) and moved from Tennessee to southern Illinois. Marion and Florence had eleven children: Lemore, Lester, and Catherine (*pictured left, left center, and right center, above*), Leonard, Cletus (*above right*), Ellen, Jennie Mae, Glenna, Charles Edward, Betty June, and John (Jennie, Charles, and Betty died in infancy). Sons Lemore, Lester, and Leonard worked in Roosevelt's Civilian Conservation Corps in the late Depression years, and Robert, Lemore, and Cletus served in the Army during World War II. Marion, who moved his family to Murphysboro in 1947, died at seventy-four years of age in 1954. Florence was eighty-one when she died in 1977. A lifelong friendship grew between Lester Milton and the author's brother Wayne during their school days at Sharon and years of working together at Springdale Orchards.

The library at Sharon was excellent. At least it seemed so to me. We had one bookcase full of books at home, but there were many shelves of books in the school library, all begging to be read. The small retreat was a prize to be won. You could raise your hand and ask permission to go to the library only if you'd finished your studies, so learning to read well in a hurry was a must. And one to be relished! We stole away into our world of books with wonder, for we were in love with learning.

Be assured that our little group was not deprived of necessary learning tools. Our library had a large dictionary. And a huge globe–we could spin it, stop it with one finger, fantasize about being in that particular country, and, if sufficiently intrigued, look up the country in the *Encyclopaedia Britannica*. We even had a copy machine called a hectograph. Ink imprints were made on paper and transferred to a tray of gelatin. Copies could then be made as needed. But, best of all, there were books. Books on the exploits of the Bobbsey Twins. And Mark Twain's *The Adventures of Tom Sawyer* and *The Adventures of Huckleberry Finn*. And Louisa May Alcott's *Little Women*. And many, many more, including extra copies of the grammar school readers, which were used by students in all eight grades. My favorite of these was a little volume called *Elson Grammar School Reader*, Book Four. Early in my road toward literacy, I was excited to learn that the English alphabet was, itself, a poem and could be recited in a sing-song fashion. As my vocabulary grew, so grew my interest in the works of America's most loved poet-writers and particularly those of Henry Wadsworth Longfellow. I was convinced then and still am that Longfellow's "Evangeline: A Tale of Acadie," with its unrhymed words so magically wed, was an incomparable literary work. As was "The Song of Hiawatha," with its enchanting images:

"By the shores of Gitche Gumee,
By the shining Big-Sea-Water, . . ."

The Book Four reader also contained works of William Cullen Bryant, John Greenleaf Whittier, Oliver Wendell Holmes, James Russell Lowell, and

Nathanial Hawthorne, as well as those of England's William Shakespeare, Percy Bysshe Shelley, Lord Byron, Robert Browning, Rudyard Kipling, and Alfred, Lord Tennyson. At age eight, I became fast friends with this host of great writers, and they fostered in me a desire to write something of my own. That desire, fed in the pastoral setting of our home place, spawned a fledgling writer.

Although poetry caught my early fancy, I liked writing other things, too. I wrote my first serious essay as a fourth grader at Sharon. I was so deeply enamored of Abraham Lincoln at the time that I thought his lean frame and melancholy face the epitome of male comeliness. In fact, historical references to his appearance as lanky or homely struck me as unfounded. I decided to write a treatise on his life and times that would lay these allegations to rest. It had to be powerful enough to convince the world that this man was truly beautiful. The piece won critical acclaim from my teacher but was not destined for posterity. Nonetheless, I learned in that exercise that words found on the printed pages of our readers could be used to express one's innermost feelings.

The actual penmanship involved in recording our thoughts was not done haphazardly. Periodic Palmar Method drills helped us develop a lovely flowing hand that could be read by one and all. Some of us never quite mastered the art.

Of course, we didn't spend all our time reading and writing. The business end of our education was mathematics. My brothers and sisters and I had all learned to count to infinity—at least a hundred—it seemed, before we started school. At school, we progressed from adding to multiplying to long division. Now, there was a challenge, especially in a Friday afternoon blackboard ciphering match! Mastering the fundamentals of mathematics was a must, and our teachers never failed us. Even I, who lit up like a small torch in my reading classes, found that problem solving could be interesting, too.

And, of course, there was the completely engrossing subject of world history where one could step back into another time at will. Learning dates was something one endured, but learning of people and places was pure adventure.

In the Cool, Cool, Cool of the Springtime

"You've got your shirt on round about—You'll have good luck the day throughout."

When we were very young, Mother quoted this little poem from some unknown source to us. It was her gentle way of teaching us how to dress ourselves. But I remember very clearly ignoring her hint and wearing my dress inside out one entire day as I expectantly waited for the promised good luck.

Along with the gentle reminders of how to dress came some more serious training in clothing construction. When Ethel and I were little more than toddlers, Mother taught us how to cut out and hand stitch quilting blocks and doll dresses from floral flour sack material. When we were big enough for our feet to reach the treadle of the sewing machine, we graduated to real dresses.

Although we had J. C. Penney, Montgomery Ward, Sears & Roebuck, Alden's, and Spiegel catalogs in our home, little girl dresses were not to be ordered. Mother was a prolific seamstress and made us many garments on the sewing machine and, sometimes, by hand. She did most of her sewing in the summertime, as I recall, when pretty cotton fabrics were plentiful at Penney's and we were available for fittings.

Wearing a new dress when school began in late summer was wonderful because it didn't have to be covered. Dressing for school in the wintertime was a different story. Any patience and ingenuity I now possess may have had beginnings in those early morning toilets. Yes, we wore them. You couldn't walk three miles to school in frigid weather without your long johns on. And remembering how embarrassing it was to have the ridge showing under your stockings is not a pleasant thing.

For us girls, the underwear came first, then a slip, then the long stockings. Then short bloomers with elasticized legs to hold up the stockings. The elastic in new bloomers was so snug that it virtually shut off the circulation in your legs so that you had to move it up and down constantly. This posed a problem for me. The bloomers were meant to show just the least little bit, but I wanted mine well out of sight. Then came oxfords or Mary Janes. Shoes, especially new ones, were not to be shuffled into carelessly. The oxfords were eased on with a shoe horn, and the straps of the Mary Janes were fastened over our firm little foundations with a buttonhook. Then came a short cotton frock matched to the bloomers. And then came a coat with woolen mittens pinned to the sleeves, and a woolen sock cap. And, finally, there were the cloth galoshes that buckled snugly over our shoes. Actually, they weren't always worn buckled. The fashionable young ladies of Chicago had started the fad of leaving a buckle or two undone so that their galoshes flapped as they walked. Somehow, the fad found its way to rural southern Illinois, and a whole new crop of "flappers," as the originals came to be called, sprang up.

Small wonder, then, that we were eager to get free of all these encumbrances in the springtime. I have a vivid recollection of walking home one fairly warm day with my underwear rolled up under my bloomers and my stockings rolled down. The breezes fairly kissed my knees! That delicious freedom, however, was not to be tasted until our mother decided the time was right. And, so, each spring there was a certain amount of intrigue, if not outright mutiny, as we waited impatiently for knee sock or anklet weather to arrive.

Of course, the ultimate was the day we could shed all our footwear and go barefoot. Shoes and socks were worn in the summertime only when we went to town, to church, or to visit our neighbors.

As I think about it now, it is apparent that our mother had a fashion sense that transcended time. For our last-day-of-school outfits one year, she bought Ethel and me boys' jeans (they didn't make them for girls then), shirts, and straw hats. Ethel and I launched the jeans craze at our all-day picnic at Riverside Park in Murphysboro. It was a first in our community, at least, and being a trendsetter was pretty heady stuff, as I recall.

Ethel reminded me of one more layer in our cold weather attire that should not be forgotten. Mother would stand at the door and dust our faces with her sweet-smelling powder as we filed past her on our way to school. An intoxicating send-off!

O Tannenbaum, Our Tannenbaum

A box supper at Sharon School was an event to be remembered. Where else could a person observe so much drama in one evening as young men, including our own Lester and George, bid outrageous sums ranging from a quarter to a dollar for the boxes of certain girls in the community? And holidays were always festive occasions. At Halloween every windowpane in the schoolhouse was plastered with witches on broomsticks and ghosts and goblins. Thanksgiving inspired another round of creative art, all duly exhibited. But Christmas was the event that really got us going.

The first order of business was sprucing up the place, and we all got into the act. Floor sweep was put down and the floors thoroughly cleaned. The windows were washed until they sparkled. Crepe paper streamers were twisted and tacked at the corners of the room and the center intersection, with a huge collapsible red bell finishing off the overhead canopy. The Christmas tree was usually brought from area woodlots by Lester or George. Then came the tour de force. Ropes of popcorn and cranberries and chains of construction paper were lovingly draped on our towering tree. Then the teacher climbed a ladder to place our tinfoil star of Bethlehem on the highest branch.

Curtains, in storage in the attic the rest of the year, were placed across the front of the room to form a stage for the performance of our annual Christmas play. Several rehearsals were in order, of course, as the excitement built toward the magic night of nights.

On one such night, we all dressed in our finest. My dress was a hand-stitched pongee (from Penney's remnant box) with a dropped waist like the flappers wore. Ethel had natural curls, but my hair had to have an assist from a curling iron. Finally, we set out in the crisp night air for the school in our sleigh—our wagon, actually. The roads were probably impassable by car, but we didn't know that.

Dad put hay to sit on and blankets to sit under in the wagon bed. The quiet trip through the hushed splendor of a starry December night was like a pilgrimage to Bethlehem and set the stage for the wonders to come.

We entered the shadowy room, lit only by a hanging oil lamp and filled with the pungent odors of the fir tree, navel oranges, and candies. The red-green streamers twisted and turned in the air currents, and we were consumed with the thrill of it all. Never mind the little hitches in our program, such as forgotten lines that required prompting or a curtain that refused to pull!

Santa Claus appeared shortly after Mr. Moore (a Sharon School Board member and father of the Moore children attending the school) disappeared, and each child got a stocking full of goodies to be hoarded at least a day or two and then enjoyed. The trip back home was negotiated in a dreamlike state you could keep for a while. Christmas was not over yet!

With my own recollection of Christmases at our house came one of my father's. He told me a wonderful story about an early Christmas when Lester and George were about five and six years old and the family was living on the Modglin farm. Dad and Mom were so financially strapped that year that there was no money to be spent for gifts. None. Dad said he wracked his brain for days trying to come up with something, anything, for the boys. One day, when he was in the shed where the potato crop was stored, two potatoes he had set aside because they were outsized and oddly shaped (like animals minus legs and tails) caught his eye. He figured with a little help they could be animals. So he fashioned two little horses, with legs and tails whittled from twigs, and wrapped them in newspapers tied up with twine. On Christmas morning Mom worked her magic in the kitchen, and Dad brought out the two bundles. Dad said the boys were as pleased with their gifts as if they had requested them and them alone.

We children never realized that times were hard. Didn't we always have a tree that towered to the top of our nine-foot ceiling? Wasn't it decorated with wonderful artwork we had made? Didn't Jack Frost decorate our windows for us with ethereal creations that made the imagination soar? And didn't each child receive a gift? That's right. We never expected more than one gift each. One memorable year, Charley got a jackknife and I got a Teddy bear. Having watched Lester and George disembowel game for the table, Charley promptly borrowed my Teddy bear, hung him by his heels, and slit his abdomen. Sometime later, I found him separated from his straw interior. I can't remember if the Teddy recovered.

I have a better memory of our Christmas feasts, though. From her rich store of canned goods in the cellar and with meat from the smokehouse, Mom made us a meal such as we had not had all year long. And afterward there were crates of oranges, fresh coconuts, peanut brittle, chocolate kisses, and assorted Christmas candies. Our time to indulge!

The wedding portrait of Robert and Laura C. Mileur Moore, made in Murphysboro in 1921. These Murphysboro Township natives (Robert was born July 16, 1896, to Thomas and Laura Graff Moore, and Laura, November 6, 1900, to Alex and Eva May Burkey Mileur) lived on their old homestead northwest of Murphysboro until it was destroyed by the 1925 tornado. They rebuilt a small place and continued to live there until 1927, when they moved to a farm southwest of Sharon School, where the family lived until 1978. Robert was a member of the school board from the late 1920s through the 1930s, when his five children—Roberta (shown in the Sharon School group in this volume), Clarence, Kenneth, Robert B., and Frederick—attended Sharon. Robert died at eighty-one years of age in 1977. The ever beautiful Laura died February 16, 1997, at ninety-six years of age. The author remembers the school days and Christmases past shared with members of this family. And Robert and Laura are the great grandparents of Justin Allen and Joshua Cale Caraway, the author's grandnephews.

On Christmas eve, as we settled down somewhat fitfully for a winter nap, strange sounds could be heard from our upstairs. But, finally, all was quiet and only a few hours separated us from magic time.

> 'Twas the night before Christmas, when all through the house
> Not a creature was stirring, not even a mouse.
>
> —Clement Moore, "A Visit from St. Nicholas"

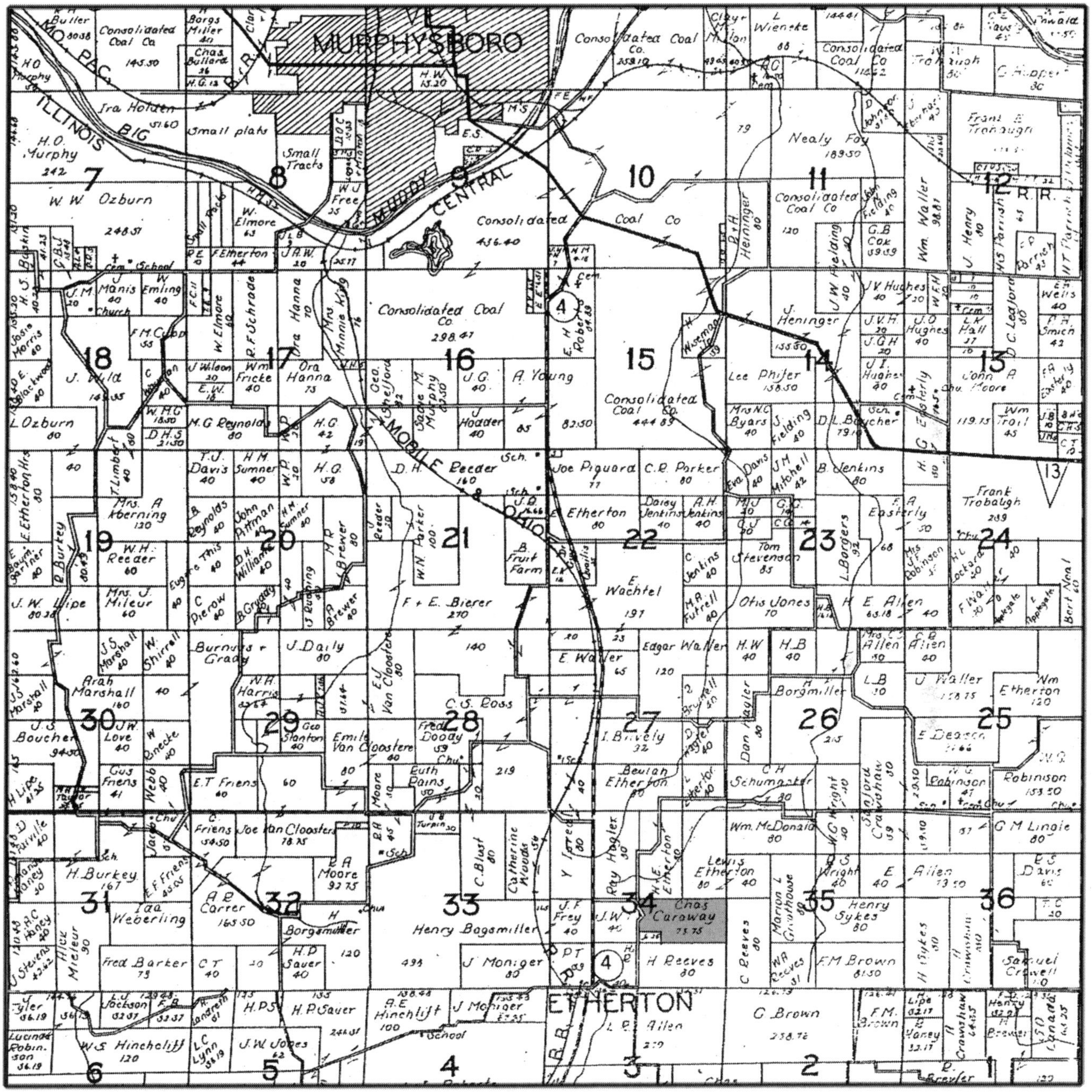

A plat map from the 1930s. The Charless Caraway farm (shaded area in lower center) appears, as do the farms of the Caraways' neighbors. (The original label of the Caraway farm, "Chas Earway," an error, has been changed in this representation.)

Take Us Out to the Ball Game

Southern Illinois has long been acknowledged as a fertile generation-to-generation breeding ground for athletes and sports fans alike. Softball and baseball were popular pastimes in many of our small towns and outlying communities at the turn of the century, but other sports, such as football and track, had followers, too. As children, we became aware of many stars of the sports world whose exploits were publicized. We knew about the great baseball pitcher Jay Hanna "Dizzy" Dean, who dominated the sport in the 1930s. We heard a great deal about Mildred "Babe" Didrikson Zaharias, who made her sports debut in 1931 and excelled at track events and many other sports. And we certainly knew about Jesse Owens, America's great African American track star, who destroyed his competition at the 1936 Olympics in Hitler's Germany.

I remember the day I saw my first real athlete. I was a preschooler gazing out a window at our home place early one morning. Ernie Davis, who lived on the nearby M&O Fruit Farm, came running down our lane in his track uniform. After that first sighting, we would watch for him and then call out, "Here he comes." This fascination with our resident runner, who was a member of Southern Illinois Normal University men's track team, grew into an admiration for all who were fleet of foot and skilled in athletic activities.

When I began school at Sharon, I learned immediately that our playground was a veritable beehive of athletic events. A multitude of activities had to be packed into our fifteen-minute recesses and one-hour lunch breaks. There were the swings, of course, and the seesaws and a merry-go-round. But by far the most interesting activities were the games associated with chants like

"Ring around a rosy,
Pocket full of posy. . . ."

Or

"Red Rover, Red Rover,
Let Cleo come over!"

And

"The farmer in the dell,
The farmer in the dell,
Hi ho, the derrio,
The farmer in the dell."

We played hide-and-seek a lot, too, and an unlikely game called pile-on-sacks in which children twirled each other around until one of them fell down. Those who fell had to hold their positions until the game was over. Crack-the-whip was an even more punishing game for the smaller child, usually at the end of the line, who was thrown across the playground as the line whipped around.

The hoop-and-paddle craze kept us rolling along to and from school, during school recesses, and after school for a while. Small metal hoops were kept upright and propelled, for those skilled in the game, by an occasional tap from the paddle. As I remember, these hoops were the iron rings that held the wooden spokes of wagon wheels in place. This fad reached such proportions that one could wonder now how many wagon wheels gave way unexpectedly for want of rims. I can't recall actually hearing of that happening, but it was a distinct possibility, given the number of hoops that were rolling around the neighborhood.

But the one sport that electrified the entire student body was a ball game. Yes, we had an actual diamond with a pitching mound, bases, and a backstop. And some fair talent. Like "Lefty" (Leona) Perrigan. When she stepped up to the mound, even the big boys gritted their teeth and called up their reserves. Because, nine times out of ten, she could strike them out. Occasionally, we had games with visiting teams from Jenkins or Rock Hill, and that was exciting. And sometimes our team piled into the teacher's car for a return engagement, just like the big leaguers.

And When We Were Bad

> My object all sublime
> I shall achieve in time—To let the punishment fit the
> crime—The punishment fit the crime.
>
> —W. S. Gilbert, *The Mikado*, act 2

I wonder what it was about Mrs. Doody that made unseemly classroom behavior unthinkable. But not all our teachers at Sharon inspired an unblemished record in deportment. And their instruments of torture—a ruler for smiting fingers and palms and a paddle with holes in it for whacking posteriors—were kept at ready and in clear view as a deterrent to crime. Occasionally, they were used on the male population, as I recall, at our little institution.

There were milder forms of punishment, of course. Like standing in the corner, confessing your sins in multiples on the blackboard, or pounding the erasers, all cruel and unusual means of punishment to my way of thinking. I remember the time a mischievous classmate, who sat behind me, tapped me on the shoulder and whispered something to me. I turned at the precise moment the teacher's eyes honed in on the disturbance. I definitely had not initiated this infraction, but talking during books was not to be countenanced, and the verdict was guilt by association. I was sentenced to a written confession (one hundred times on tablet paper). To this day, I am a firm believer in the "innocent until proven guilty" adage.

Of course, there was the matter of punishment for infractions incurred at home. A couple of stories concerning Dad's total failure as a stern disciplinarian have been told and retold in our family. In one instance, Dad picked up three-year-old Wayne and gave him a firm spat on his backside for some misdeed. Wayne promptly wrapped his chubby little arms around Dad's neck and said, "Daddy, don't pat me so hard." In the other, young Charley was spanked for tarrying too long in Mr. Ross's pasture on his way home from school. With all the dignity he could muster under the circumstances, Charley deposited his prize possession—a pocket knife—at Dad's feet and walked away. The effect was shattering! Dad never again attempted any form of corporal punishment. But one look of disapproval from him, or from Mother or one of the boys, was sufficient to quell any notion of illicit behavior!

Part Two ❧ Wildwood Days

We Strolled the Lane Together

> When daisies pied and violets blue
> And lady-smocks all silver-white
> And cuckoo-buds of yellow hue
> Do paint the meadows with delight.
>
> —Shakespeare, *Love's Labour's Lost,* act 5, scene 2

Our mother had a green thumb, and the fruits of her labors were bounty to feed the body and beauty to feed the soul. But her love of plant life extended beyond her gardens to the wildlands, and our summer excursions with her over meadow and into the wood awakened in us the same lifelong affinity with Nature that she had. As we followed our guide, we searched in vain for elusive four-leaf clovers while she found one for each of us, chewed tangy pennyroyal leaves, sniffed wild roses, listened to the legend of the scarred petals of the dogwood, jumped over Johnny-jump-ups, and strolled through fields of daisies in happy abandon.

Sometimes we set out on deliberate missions. At least once every spring, we would take along a hoe so Mom could grub out some sassafras roots for tea that not only tasted good but also purified our systems. In the summer, there were plump wild blackberries to be gathered for cobblers. In the fall, there were hazelnuts, walnuts, and hickory nuts to gather and ripe, sweet persimmons to eat on the spot! And, occasionally, from the deep, black earth of our nearby woodlands, we brought back wild ferns to be domesticated.

Farther afield, plants like the tiger lily, the cattail, the crowfoot, foxtail grass, the bachelor's button, the lady-slipper, Queen Anne's lace, and the weeping willow generated more than a passing interest. The pussy willow came in for some very close scrutiny. Our *Elson Reader,* Book One, had a picture of real little kittens poised on willow shoots. When we came across a clump of willows one day that had just sprouted balls of fur, I asked my mother as nonchalantly as possible if they would grow into kittens. She assured me that they would not, but I decided they would bear watching anyway.

You simply couldn't miss some plants because of their colors. Who could forget a southern Illinois woodland with its most flamboyant species—black gum, sweet gum, red maple, sugar maple, oak hickory, ash, sumac, and sassafras—all dressed in their autumn finery? Some species, like the glorious redbud and the enchanting bluebell, were harbingers of spring. The black-eyed Susans of summer were really impressive, and the amazing thing about these plants was that they could tell if you were jealous. You simply held one under the chin—if the yellow reflected onto the skin's surface, you were jealous, indeed!

There were some plants that elicited great respect for the marvelous way they got your attention, like the winged seeds of the maple, the oak's acorns with their snug little tasseled berets, the nuts of the hazel with their cleverly ruffled encasements, and the milkweeds whose stems secreted a milky juice.

Then there were the beggar's-lice and cockleburs that insisted on coming home with you after every summer outing. And they weren't the only unwanted souvenirs. Ethel came down once with a severe case of poison oak. Her face swelled so badly that she had to be fed through a straw for several days. Mother treated her with a baking soda poultice, and she finally got better. Her face peeled completely so that in the midsummer, when we were usually tanned brown as the proverbial berry, she had skin as soft and white as a baby's. I thought it was almost worth the agony.

But these occasional setbacks did nothing to dampen our enthusiasm for our outings, and our mother continued to stroll the lanes and backwoods with us and instill in us, with her bits of knowledge and whimsy, a fascination for plant life that has lasted through the years. Almost any occasion could be turned into a special event, like an impromptu visit to Etherton Switch to visit the Sherwood family who lived there. It was just a hop, skip, and a jump to Etherton if you

Cynthia Belle Brown and Finus Rufus Doy Sherwood, known as Belle and Doy, and their six younger children at their home place in Etherton Switch in 1928, with their new Chevrolet touring car in the background. In the front row (*left to right*) are Woodrow, Buford, Mildred, Mary Ellen, and Rufus. In the back row are Doy, Belle, and baby, Billie Dean. The two elder daughters, Verda and Eva, were already married when this photograph was taken. The first child, Carle Odell, died in infancy. Belle and Doy were married in rural Tennessee on October 7, 1906, when they were fifteen and sixteen years of age. Doy, of Irish ancestry and an employee of the Mobile and Ohio Railroad, was transferred from central Tennessee to southern Illinois (Unity, in Alexander County) in 1922. Two years later he was promoted to section foreman for the M&O at Etherton Switch, about seven miles south of Murphysboro on Route 127. The family lived in the village of Etherton until Doy was transferred to Alto Pass in 1940. Doy died in 1974 at eighty-four years of age. Belle was eighty-six when she died three years later. Members of the Caraway and Sherwood families visited one another regularly during the 1930s.

walked cater-corner through the neighbor's pastureland that lay between our place and the village. On the way, there were rocks and rills and green-clad hills that were new to us and begging to be explored. And Mother picked a time when we didn't have to hurry.

For one wonderful summer, we lucky children had as our next-door neighbor another delightful Irish lady who liked to explore our environs as much as Mother did. Hiking down the road to "Claudie" Bodkin's house was special! Her meticulous home was a treasure trove of handicraft. Her specialty was fine needlework, but it was her quilting that got my undivided attention. After we'd looked at her latest projects and enjoyed some of her delicious tidbits, Claudie would take us for a stroll.

We younger children were not the only ones who liked tramping about. Lester and George sometimes went on hiking excursions near and far beyond the confines of our family farm with their friends. One Sunday afternoon they visited Flat Rock Cave on the old Bierer fruit farm, occupied long ago by area Indians and more recently by hoboes and fugitives from the law, and made mulligan stew in its courtyard. They roamed farther afield, too, to places like Little Grand Canyon or the Pomona Natural Bridge, and listening to their stories about these places was almost as good as being there.

Occasionally, Grandpa would take his cane and strike out across the pastures and fields on his own.

Claudia "Claudie" McKnight Bodkin and her baby son, Robert Eugene, in 1939 when the family lived at their home place atop Tomcat Hill, south of Etherton Switch. Claudia was born in Johnstonville, Tennessee, December 8, 1902. She and Robert Ira Bodkin, both of Irish descent and reared in a community near Fruitland, Tennessee, eloped by train September 8, 1919, to a neighboring town to get married. An employee of the Mobile and Ohio Railroad, Bob brought Claudia and their firstborn son, James Oscar, to southern Illinois in 1923. In the mid-1930s, the Bodkins lived for about a year on the Modglin place and established lifelong friendships with members of the author's family. Bob died January 24, 1979, at seventy-three years of age. Claudia lived at the farm until she was eighty-four. She died October 18, 1997, at ninety-four.

I have a suspicion he was walking in memories with his beloved "Viney," because he was always strangely quiet when he returned from these treks.

And, once in a while, Mom and Dad would set out on their own, too. There was a tacit understanding that we children were not to tag along on these occasions. Mom might issue a few simple instructions, and off they'd go. Years later, when I found a poem by Mildred S. Andrews, "I Took One Final Walk across the Fields," among Mother's keepsakes, I knew she had clipped it while remembering the private moments she and Dad had shared during their strolls. Here are the first two stanzas of the poem:

> I took one final walk across the fields
> To where the pasture meets the little wood,
> I passed the gap to climb the homestead hill
> And on the little promontory stood.
> How often have we two together made
> The same excursion for a better cause:
> To fetch a calf, to mend a broken fence,
> To watch the grazing cattle as we pause.

Lester (*seated, with hat in hand*) and George Caraway (*standing, second from left*) and members of their social set from the Mount Pleasant Methodist Church on a summer day in 1933, when they picnicked at Little Grand Canyon. This scenic area became part of the Shawnee National Forest when it was established in southern Illinois that same year. The forest, named for the Shawnee Indians who hunted in the area as modern history began, now stretches across southern Illinois from the Mississippi River to the Ohio and abounds in towering rock formations, peaceful rivers and streams, and historic sites that include ancient Indian walls and the caves they used, all encompassed in forested rolling hills replete with wildlife.

Thought I'd Drop You a Line

Our somewhat remote location did not, as some might suspect, separate us from the outside world. We had a number of excellent sources of current information. With some regularity, we inherited copies of the *Saturday Evening Post*, *Colliers*, the *Ladies Home Journal*, and other magazines, all of which were devoured. But we subscribed to the *Daily Independent* and the *Prairie Farmer*, and we purchased the *Old Farmer's Almanac* annually. These three publications were considered essential to our existence.

The *Daily Independent* was our means of keeping up with happenings in Murphysboro and the exploits of comic strip and cartoon characters like Alley Oop and Flapper Fannie. And important celebrities like the Dionne quintuplets. These identical girl babies, born in an isolated log farmhouse near Callander, Ontario, Canada, on May 28, 1934, had our close attention from that day forward. After all, this was something described by doctors as unprecedented in the history of mankind, and we, along with the rest of the world, eagerly followed their day-to-day development. And we greatly admired Dr. Dafoe, who had kept the miracle babies alive by warming them at the oven door of a wood-burning stove just like ours and by stimulating them with brandy from an eyedropper! And, of course, there were the child movie stars like Shirley Temple and Jane Withers, who fascinated us even though we had never seen them in their movies. I was quite impressed with these young stars and clipped their photographs religiously. But my collection met with disaster when our pet hen, who occasionally darted into the house through an open screen door, used my box of clippings for a nest (most of my prize photos were scratched to shreds, creased from her weight, or permanently stuck to her eggs). And we didn't neglect the glamorous older stars, such as Jean Harlow, who managed to get their pictures in our newspaper.

The *Old Farmer's Almanac*, "published every year since 1792," hung on its own string from a nail in the kitchen wall (the publisher thoughtfully provides a hole in the upper left corner for this very purpose). It was consulted regularly for predicted weather patterns, recommended planting cycles, et cetera. I mean, you wouldn't think of planting precious seeds without paying heed to the *Almanac.*

But the *Prairie Farmer* had a special status in our home, as did a lovely little trunk that had belonged to our grandmother, Johanna. The trunk had, on the interior of the arched lid, a picture of a beautiful, furry kitten who looked like one of our very own; and it contained treasures that we liked to take out, look at, and put back every so often. Occasionally, Mom would dispense something special from her store. Like the old and elegant valentines she gave Ethel and Wayne when they told her one morning that the other children would be exchanging cards that day (the cards were taken to school and given to the same person—Roberta Moore). But the trunk also served as a correspondence compartment. You see, our mother belonged to the *Prairie Farmer* Pen Pal Club. She corresponded with farm women all over the nation and even abroad and at one time had the bottom portion of the trunk nearly full of letters from her pen pals. I recall the great excitement of the day we got a shipment of English boxwood (a species once reserved for royalty) from a correspondent across the sea. The shrubs were promptly planted in front of the house, and they began to grow immediately as if to prove that they could look regal anywhere. But Mom's favorite pen pal was "Birdy" from Arkansas. Mom and Birdy sent locks of baby hair, swatches of fabric, and, occasionally, unusual mementos as they wrote each other about their children, home and garden projects, et cetera. Birdy once sent Mom a cotton seed. Mom planted it in the back yard, and soon we had a cotton plant, too.

Tell Us Why the Stars Do Shine

Twinkle, twinkle, little star!
How I wonder what you are,
Up above the world so high,
Like a diamond in the sky!
—Ann Taylor, *The Star*

Scientists now tell us that interstellar dust from distant, dying stars is sprinkled with diamonds. So the ancients, who thought diamonds were splinters from stars, were diviners of a great truth. But long before I knew this, and certainly before I learned that pockets of air in the atmosphere bend the light from stars to make them appear to twinkle, I was convinced that the stars were diamonds in the sky. And a fascination with the heavenly bodies began.

On summer evenings, we children sometimes sat at the back door stoop and sang, appropriately, the chorus from "K-K-K-Katy":

When the m-m-m-moon shines,
Over the cowshed,
I'll be waiting at the k-k-k-kitchen door.

Then Mother would point out the various celestial configurations like the Big Dipper and the Little Dipper and the bright expanse of the Milky Way. Often in her discourses, Mother would admonish us to "Hitch your wagon to a star" (the admonishment stuck with me, and years later I traced it to Ralph Waldo Emerson's "Civilization," an essay from *Society and Solitude*, 1870). She taught us, too, how to make a secret wish. Thereafter, I would make nightly pilgrimages out-of-doors, look up and zero in on one star, cross my fingers, and recite

Star light, star bright,
First star I see tonight,

I wish I may, I wish I might
Have the wish I wish tonight.

I know now that, according to astronomer Carl Sagan, there are ten billion trillion stars and that we can only see about five thousand of them with the naked eye. On those not-so-long-ago summer evenings, though, it seemed to me that every star in the heavens clustered around our hilltop for the sole purpose of dazzling us children. Only once did the heavenly lights present themselves to us in a manner that was frightening. One wintry night we were treated to the luminous phenomenon of the aurora borealis. We were sure something terrible was about to happen. Dad came out to take a look and told us calmly that it was only the northern lights. And we were satisfied.

I have an exquisite memory of one falling star, blazing a trail of molten stardust across the sky as it fell, seemingly, somewhere in our back forty. The sky trails from the man-made fireworks we saw each year, as we celebrated our nation's birthday at Riverside Park in Murphysboro, were *almost* like molten stardust. This spectacle, watched each July 4 from a blanket in the natural amphitheater at Riverside, has to be yet another tribute to our mother. I can see her there, thoroughly enjoying the rare outing, and not deterred in the least by the fact that she had children leaning on her from every side. But I liked the real stars better. They were not noisy.

All that I know
Of a certain star
Is, it can throw
(Like the angled spar)
Now a dart of red,
Now a dart of blue;
Till my friends have said
They would fain see, too,
My star that dartles the red and the blue!

Then it stops like a bird; like a flower, hangs furled:
They must solace themselves with the Saturn above it.
What matter to me if their star is a world?
Mine has opened its soul to me; therefore I love it.
—Robert Browning, "My Star"

Cool, Clear Water

Our rain barrels were lovely to yell down when they were empty. That meant, though, that water for many uses as well as for drinking would have to be carried up the hill from our well. We made a game of the chore, chanting

Jack and Jill went up the hill
To fetch a pail of water,
Jack fell down and broke his crown,
And Jill came tumbling after.

The only trouble was, we had to carry the full pails *up* the hill.

Still, I have only the fondest memories of that rock-lined well. I even remember the day when seventeen-year-old George lined its depths with the stones that would work wonders for us for years to come. In the summers, Mom kept her yeast (and anything else she wanted to preserve) in Ball jars in the cooling depths. A chain was attached to facilitate the tricky business of lowering and raising the jars. Otherwise, we would have lost the precious contents and had a well full of broken glass besides.

I can still taste the pure, sweet water from that well (we didn't have to worry about pollutants then). It bubbled up from an underground spring and met all our needs for many years. Not until we remodeled our house in the summer of 1938 did we have another, more convenient water system. A cistern was constructed at the back of the house to catch the roof runoff, and the trip to fetch water was shortened considerably.

By the Shore, By the Shore

The year was 1927, and the dry spell hung on. The creeks were down, and the cattle needed water. Finally, Dad decided to dam up one end of the natural hollow in the ridgetop that lay across the creek back of the house so we would have a reservoir in the event that rain did come. He and Lester and George, with a team of horses and a scoop shovel, built the dam in their "spare" time that summer.

Dad told me shortly before he died that he sat at the site a long while the day the dam was finished, wondering if their work had been an exercise in futility. The sun was scorching the earth, the sky was cloudless, and no rain was forecast. Some of the neighbors had voiced fears of their own particular plights to Dad. He said his mind had dwelt on the dire situation of the entire drought-stricken area. Later, he was convinced that his universal concern accounted for the miracle that occurred. Suddenly, a small cloud drifted across the horizon from out of nowhere and hung directly over the excavation and rained until it was full. Dad swore that there was not even a sprinkle beyond the immediate boundaries of the hilltop hollow.

Well! The cows and horses had a watering hole. We had a pond. And soon we had fish and turtles. And an occasional snake who was allowed unimpeded passage before our dips continued.

It became apparent to me, by the time I was about four years old, that Lester and George had a fun-loving social set. They decided to throw a watermelon party at the pond site. I recall the moonlit summer evening and the bright cabanas that dotted the "beachfront." As I hung about the fringes of the festivities, it was clear that this was a big-people's party (Laverne Fleming, Naomi Lingle, the Byars, the Deasons, and Ernie Davis were there). And, my goodness, they were having a great time!

Of course, we younger children had our own beach parties, too, and sometimes without proper supervision. There was the day that Betty disappeared in the shallows and finally came up with a nose full of mud. We nearly finished her off by beating on her frantically to clear her nostrils. A hasty retreat from this narrow escape seemed in order, so we opted to take the short cut (as the crow flies) home. Ordinarily, we kept to the wagon trail down the more gentle southerly slope of the hill, but the steeper westerly slope led straight down one hill, across the creek, and up another hill to the house. With Betty firmly in hand, we made a headlong dash down the hill. A large tree trunk lay smack in our chosen path. The object, of course, was to sail right over it, but Betty's three-year-old legs didn't make it, and she fell across the log with a thud that knocked the wind out of her. For a long, frightening moment, we thought she was dead. Then she gasped hoarsely, which was even more frightening. Finally, she started screaming at the top of her lungs. We struggled up the hill with a dozen "explanations" in mind, knowing full well that none of them would do. There were no more unchaperoned trips to the pond, but we were never refused a swim when we asked. Mom sat on the banks many a scorching afternoon with never a complaint and kept an eye on us as we splashed in the cooling waters until we grew weary or our skin began to pucker. As we headed for the safety of the banks, she would take a quick dip before we all traipsed along home.

But our pond was not just a warm-weather spa. When it froze over in the winter, we had an ideal outdoor skating rink. Lester and George had skates and became quite skillful on the ice. We younger children did not have skates, but some pretty fancy footwork could be negotiated without them. And, when Lester and George weren't around, we tied their skates on our feet and gave it a rather wobbly go. Nothing more serious than an occasional turned ankle occurred.

And in the summers, of course, there was another sport to indulge in. In *Fishing Southern Illinois*, published in the Shawnee Books series by the Southern Illinois University Press, author Art Reid tells us of the joys of fishing in Illinois waters. Mother would have loved Art's book for the simple reason that she loved to fish. Claude Endicott of De Soto, Illinois, a former resident of Makanda, told me a story of how his parents and my parents, who were all living in Makanda Township at the time, went fishing at Round Hole (a natural basin that retained water when the rest of the creek ran dry) on Sunday afternoons before the Country Club Lake was built. Claude was only five years old at the time, and my brothers, Lester and George, were three and two, but these fishing excursions were important events in their young lives and those of their parents.

Years later at our home place, with five more children and all the attendant responsibilities, our mother still loved to fish. Whenever she could, she would rig up lines from sturdy limbs, pieces of cord, bobbers, and hooks for herself and any of us children who wished to accompany her, and we would all sit calmly on the dam at the pond site. But before one could fish, there was the harvesting of the earthworms (we called them "wiggleworms") from beneath rocks. And then came the threading of the protesting little creatures onto the hook (mine seemed to all but spit in my eyes as they sacrificed themselves for my pastime). But throwing the line out and settling in for the occasional catch almost made up for the earlier unpleasantness. Sometimes, when the objective was fresh fish for supper and not a leisurely afternoon at water's edge, we simply waded through the shallows with a seine (an old lace curtain) in tow. I can still see the huge perch I seined out of that pond that would not fit in my gallon bucket!

Always on the lookout for daring projects, Wayne and Charley decided one day on a construction job of their own. They moved their material to a secret site in the woods and began disappearing after supper each evening. A short time later they brought up their surprise: a flatboat with oars. It floated when launched, and our pond (a small lake, actually) had a boat for navigating the waters!

Hear the Wind Blow, Dear

I hear the wind among the trees
Playing celestial symphonies . . .
—Longfellow, *A Day of Summer*

Funny thing. I do not remember actually suffering with the heat on our hilltop. We seemed always to have a breeze. I recall the explicit joy of drifting off to sleep in front of open windows with summer-clad trees soughing in the night winds.

And when a rainstorm was brewing, we children loved to race the length of the driveway headlong into the fragrant wind. It was like being embraced with long, flowing arms. I think that was when my love affair with the universe began.

But old "Maria" did not always come in with sweet-smelling breath and a gentle rain. During a big blow in 1933, I remember watching Mom determinedly holding the felt-backed wallpaper on the dining room wall as the winds threatened to peel it right off. Worse than this, the roof of our barn was lifted and carried into a neighboring field. The rest of the old barn collapsed, causing panic among the animals sheltered there. It was a major catastrophe for us, and in the aftermath George stepped on a board with a nail in it. Mom treated him and he went on about his business. Of course, we had to have a new barn. And watching it go up was just about all the excitement we could handle.

I remember one summer day when a storm swept through the countryside and left a lovely rainbow in its wake with one end trailing off behind a nearby hill. Mother, repeating the legend of the pot of gold at the end of the rainbow, suggested that we go take a look. Along the way, of course, we forgot about the pot of gold and concentrated on the wonders of the renewed earth.

In Our Merry Fordmobile

On rainy days, Dad would sometimes come to pick us up at school with a team of horses and a wagon with a big tarp in the bed for us to get under. Dad, of course, sat up front on the wagon seat and handled the team expertly with a click of the tongue and a tug of the reins. We children usually had our heads sticking out around the edges of the tarp as we tried to outdo each other adding up the numbers on the telephone poles. It never occurred to me then, but this fun exercise was excellent for sharpening our math skills for the occasional Friday afternoon ciphering match at school. And I have no idea how well we did in our calculations, either. Dad never, ever interrupted us, preferring, in his now-apparent wisdom, to let us use our own ingenuity in livening up the slow trip home.

I can't remember going to Murphysboro in our wagon, though. But George assures me that, in those early years, we did use the wagon or our buggy to make the seven-mile trip regularly from our lane north on Route 127 and west on then Route 13. I do have a faint recollection of parking at either Edwards's or Berger's hardware stores. And I recall quite clearly seeing our neighbors coming by, on their way in, comfortably ensconced on the springboard seat of their wagon. Some folks continued to use their buggies long after cars became common. I remember passing our neighbor, Jake Rendleman, as he made his way from the Bierer farm to town in his elegant black buggy. I also remember that our interest in the trips to town increased as we traveled over the bridge crossing the Big Muddy River and then under the viaduct carrying the railroad over the street. We hoped, of course, that we would roll under the train just as it rolled over us. I don't recall that it ever happened.

I will never forget the first ride I took in a car. Mr. and Mrs. Al Stotlar came down for a visit (they lived about midway between our house and town on Route 127 in the Jenkins School District). As many as could piled in their car, and away we went. I sat on Mrs. Stotlar's lap. I nearly jumped out of my skin from the unexpected sound as another car whooshed past us on the highway. Mrs. Stotlar laughed and held me tightly. I felt safe there but sorry, nonetheless, that I had come along.

Our first automobile was a very smart 1927 Model T Ford. Then we had a 1928 Model A Ford with isinglass snap-in windows. Lester broke it in by driving it to the Chicago World's Fair (the Century of Progress Exposition opened April 29, 1933, at Northerly Island, built exclusively for the fair). There is an interesting story in connection with that trip. George, always enterprising, had gone to northern Illinois to earn some extra money in the harvests. He had left his car (he owned the Model A by virtue of the fact that he had bought out Dad's stock in it) at home. He was standing on a street corner in Chicago, thumbing a ride home, when Lester and three of their friends (Ernest and Russell Deason and Johnny Byars), who were returning from the fair, drove up. George was so furious with Lester for taking his car without permission that he refused to ride home with them. It was one of the few times there was ever any friction between Lester and George, and it was not a major fracas at that. Lester was well aware that there was only one solution and soon had a car of his own, a 1929 Model A Ford Roadster with a rumble seat.

I remember one Sunday when we all piled into the Model A to go all the way to Grand Tower to picnic on the shores of the Mississippi River. We ate fish fresh from the river fried by our mother on the

The 1927 Model T Ford (the family's first car), the author (age four), Charley (age two), and Billy (the family's pet goat). George, the family shutterbug (his camera had cost him one coon pelt), captured the star of the photograph (Billy) perfectly. Billy furnished the "horsepower" for Charley's miniature farm wagon, which Lester built for him, complete with harness and shafts for turning. When Billy balked at the job, Lester attached an ear of corn to a pole for Charley to dangle just beyond his reach. Of course, Lester had to stay close to the conveyance to keep Billy from veering off the beaten path with his young passenger.

spot. After dinner George decided to go rowing in what appeared to me to be a very small boat for such a big river. I recall, vividly, the terror that gripped me as a squall came up and George had to use all his strength to maneuver the boat through the choppy waters to the shore. I could scarcely believe that he had proved to be stronger than the river!

I find I have many fond memories of the first two cars. The ones that came later are a blur at best.

When Irish Eyes Were Smiling

Winter, spring, summer, or fall. It didn't matter. When Mother's cousins from Jonesboro and points south came for a visit, good times were in store. And they came fairly often, considering that it was, at that time, a fair distance to travel.

In the summer of 1928, when I was three years old, Uncle Mike Kelley (the brother of our maternal grandmother Johanna) died, and Aunt Belle (his wife) immediately assumed the role of matriarch of the clan. Aunt Belle's daughters, Delia Lingle and Maude Knupp, and June, Maude's daughter, came that summer for the first visit that I can remember. They came by train to Etherton Switch and then walked the half mile or so up the road and across the field to our place. June, about five years old at the time, thought the train ride interminable and hazardous, too—rocks from the roadbed kept striking the windows as they sped down the track at what seemed a very fast pace. They stayed a couple of days that trip, and then Elvis, Maude's husband, came in the car to take them home.

The family's second car, a 1928 Model A Ford, and the two chauffeurs, Lester and George. The author's father, Charless, determined, after one attempt, that he would leave the driving to others. When their older brothers married and moved away, Wayne and Charley took over.

There was always a mad scramble to make sleeping arrangements for our guests, but we managed very well. And sleeping at the foot of the bed or in more or less neat rows of five crosswise in the bed was a small price to pay to see our mother's Irish eyes smiling with the joy of having her own kinfolk there. Through the years of Mother's youth, to her mother's early death at Makanda, Illinois, to the time of her marriage and move to Murphysboro Township, she

Aunt Belle and Uncle Mike (Jessie Isabelle Smiddy and Michael Thomas Kelley) at a farm they rented near Jonesboro, Illinois, for a time. Mike and his sisters—Kathleen, Johanna (the author's maternal grandmother), and Fannie—were the children of Thomas Sean and Lena Kathrine Pierce Kelley, who came to America from Ireland in the mid-1800s at the time of the Great Potato Famine. Mike was born in Rock Island, Illinois, August 31, 1867, and moved with his family to Union County when he was three years old. He and Belle were married June 16, 1890.

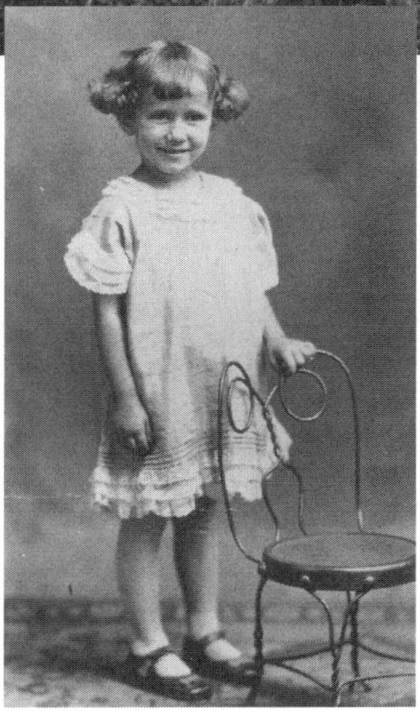

Mike and Belle Kelley (*seated*) at their farm in Anna Township, with a portrait of their deceased daughter, Fannie June, between them and their surviving children behind them (*left to right*: Delia Lillian, William Thomas, Maude Adeline, Raymond McDonald, and Francis Lester). Uncle Mike died April 22, 1928, at sixty-one years of age, not long after this photograph was taken. Aunt Belle died December 28, 1958, at eighty-eight.

A formal portrait of Cousin June Knupp (granddaughter of Mike and Belle Kelley and daughter of Elvis and Maude Kelley Knupp), who took her first and rather frightening train ride from Jonesboro to Etherton Switch with her mother and aunt in 1928 to visit the author's family.

hadn't seen her relatives. The family had scattered for various reasons, and they came together, finally, in a conscious effort to make up for the years of separation and deprivation.

With Aunt Belle, the making up was easy. She was a delight! About five feet tall, she was an absolute bundle of bustling energy who gave everybody who came within range a firm hug and a kiss. Watching her comb out her glorious hair (it had never been cut) in the mornings and twist it up into a shining coil on top of her head was an event I tried not to miss. And she didn't seem to mind my gaping, giving me a quick hug and kiss as soon as she finished. She and her daughters, Delia and Maude, were witty and wonderful Irish ladies to the hilt. And how our mother loved them all!

In the summer of 1938, the whole clan (or most of it) gathered at our house for a Sunday fest. And this time, Aunt Kate Kelley Sitter (a sister of our Grandmother Johanna and Great-Uncle Mike) came, too. This was one of the few times we ever saw Aunt Kate. She was a memorable lady, too, but not so ready to show her affection as Aunt Belle. But Mom loved her as well; and years later, when Aunt Kate died, Mom was the recipient of some elegant antique furniture from her estate.

I recall with great nostalgia now the Sunday mornings when we would make a spur-of-the-moment decision to visit members of the Kelley clan in their own bailiwick. The gatherings were generally at the Knupp farm with cousins, cousins everywhere. Mother loved being with her people and went to great lengths to gather the clan even after she fell ill. Ethel once voiced her concern to Dad when Mom began to plan her usual Christmas dinner for our large family and the Kelleys who could come. After a long pause, he said, "The ability to perform is governed by desire. She desires."

As I began writing this chapter of *Growing Up in a Land Called Egypt*, I resurrected a story that I had clipped from the June 19, 1988, issue of *Parade Magazine* ("Where You Can Discover Your Past"). The article declared, "Your name–and almost every other name ever recorded on earth–will likely be on file one day at the Mormon Family History Library in Salt Lake City." This declaration inspired me to start a search of our Kelley ancestors and then prepare a genealogy called *The Kelley Clan (Descendants of an Emigrant from the Emerald Isle)*.

Elsewhere in this book there are stories of migrations of diverse people from many European nations to America. As I assembled information for my genealogy, long-told anecdotes and newfound facts came together in yet another marvelous tale of two continents. A condensed version of the introduction to my saga of our Kelley ancestors follows:

My maternal great-grandparents left Ireland via the back door of their Dublin blacksmith shop as British soldiers came in the front in the mid-1800s. Thomas Sean and Lena Kathrine Pierce Kelley left their baby, Mary, who was ill, with relatives, made their way to the harbor, and surreptitiously boarded a ship bound for America. The stowaways were not discovered until the ship was midocean. In America, Thomas and Kathrine came across the country by covered wagon to Rock Island, Illinois, a railroad center. The family moved to Anna, Illinois, in 1870. Thomas, some years later, left his wife and four children—Kathleen Ann, Michael Thomas, Johanna (our maternal grandmother), and Fannie—in Anna to seek his fortune in the Black Hills gold rush. He died in Central City, South Dakota, January 8, 1880, in a typhoid fever and pneumonia epidemic that swept through his mining camp, and he was buried in the Catholic cemetery at Deadwood, South Dakota. Kathrine and her four children survived somehow, and, to date, my research has recorded well over one hundred descendants.

Now I have a wonderful series of footnotes to this story. In the course of researching our Irish ancestry, I and members of our family were always aware of an inexplicable longing to actually see the land of our mother's heritage. In the year 2000, Ethel's grandson, U.S. Navy seaman John McFarland Alexander Miller (the great-great-great-grandson of Thomas and Kate Kelley), made a pilgrimage to the Emerald Isle. John went on long walking tours and spent two days in Dublin's harbor with two old fishermen. Once, when he asked strangers for directions to a hotel, they took him home with them to spend the night. In 2001 Betty and her two daughters (Laura Marie and Linda Susan Nettland, the great-great-granddaughters of Thomas and Kate) boarded an Aer Lingus flight to blaze a trail in the "wild blue yonder" to Ireland. Their Irish heritage tour took them to castles and cottages, coastal cliffs, rivers and lakes and mountains, unequaled pastoral scenes, and fabled Irish pubs. One memorable evening Laura and Linda, who are active members of a theatrical productions group, were invited to join the entertainers in Ceili dancing at the Laurels Pub in Killarney. On their own on a "soft" (rainy) afternoon, as their tour drew to a close, they went by cab to St. Mary's Catholic Church in Dublin, where Thomas was baptized April 23, 1841 (data from the Dublin Heritage Group Baptism Database). At the exact moment Laura and Linda disembarked from the cab, the bells of St. Mary's welcomed them to the city of their ancestry. Laura captured the magical sights and sounds of the beautiful old church on her camcorder for all of us to see and hear. Then, in 2002, Betty and Laura made a second journey back in time to visit the St. Ambrose Catholic Church and Cemetery in Deadwood, South Dakota, to try to find Thomas's burial plot. Tombstone inscriptions in the old section of the cemetery were no longer legible, but old church records confirmed that Thomas died January 8, 1880, at Central City and was buried at St. Ambrose's Cemetery January 9.

So the Emerald Isle is calling still to the descendants of its native son and daughter and is waiting to weave its magic spell around all who come "home." For now, our own fair land and Ireland still hold secrets hidden from us in time and distance. Our search continues.

Beautiful, Beautiful Black Eyes

My sister Ethel told me a story about her granddaughter Molly. When Molly was still quite small, her friend from down the street came for a visit and brought along a little black girl she knew. The children played happily all afternoon. When it was time for the visitors to leave, Molly said to her friend, "I love your little dark sister."

Ethel's story brought to mind another incident from the past. We older children were trailing along after our mother in downtown Murphysboro one Saturday. Mother was holding the hand of our baby Betty. Just as we came even with an African American lady who was holding her baby's hand, Betty broke away and made a beeline for the beautiful little black girl. She put her arms around the baby lovingly and vocalized her pleasure at finding another person just her size. The two startled mothers looked at one another, laughed and tried to separate their children. But Betty indicated that she intended to take the baby home with her. I was very interested in these proceedings because Betty was quite adept at getting her way. It was not to be.

The object of this story is to establish the total lack of prejudice in our home. There were very few African American families in our surrounding communities. The one black gentleman we knew, Ferdinand Woods, came to our farm to work occasionally (area farmers competed for his services because he was an honest, hardworking man). He lived on a small family farm in the Bostick Settlement that lay near our place and adjacent to Mr. Ross's pastureland. His parents, White and Catherine Bostick Woods, were former slaves in Tennessee who came to southern Illinois after the Civil War. The Bostick Settlement, where Ferdinand grew up with his seven brothers and sisters—Charlotte, Mary Jane, Catherine, Melissa Ann, Charles, Abbie Everline, and Anderson—consisted of several African American families, including the Bosticks (who established the community in the late 1860s), the Woods, the Lightles, and others.

The children of these early settlers were all educated at home because there was no school for them to attend. (A school, a small church, and a private cemetery were established as the settlement grew.) As part of their early training, Catherine taught her daughters to do fine needlework in the evenings when the farm work was done. Three of the Woods sisters—Mary Jane, Melissa, and Abbie—later attended Southern Illinois University and taught in Illinois schools for many years.

The Bostick Cemetery honor roll lists four Bostick brothers—Dudley, Stephen, William, and Hardin—who served as coal passers on the frigate U.S.S. *General Bragg* during the Civil War. This intriguing bit of information created a bit of a mystery: why would these Union veterans have served on a ship obviously named for Confederate general Braxton Bragg? The *American Heritage Picture History of the Civil War*, with narrative by Bruce Catton, informed me that this ship was a prewar Mississippi side-wheeler. As a Confederate gunboat, the *General Bragg* was sunk by the Union Navy in 1862. It was later raised and outfitted with a thirty-two-pound pivot gun and reconverted into the federal gunboat on which the Bosticks served. The Bostick brothers are profiled in *Forgotten Soldiers: Murphysboro's African American Civil War Veterans* by P. M. Jones and his 1993–94 Murphysboro Middle School sixth-grade class. Much of the Woods family history was carefully recorded in a large, elegantly bound Bible published in 1874 by the American Bible Society, now a cherished possession of Charlotte Woods's granddaughter, Earlene Douglass Sanders of Murphysboro, who is a Caraway family friend.

Although there were few African Americans in our community, several members of the race got our attention in the 1930s: the boxer Joe "the Brown Bomber" Louis, the baseball star LeRoy "Satchel" Paige, the famous stage and film actor Paul Robeson, and the dancer Bill "Bojangles" Robinson, to name a few. I recall one evening when Wayne walked with his friend, Rufus Sherwood, to Etherton Switch, when we didn't have a radio that worked, to listen to one of Louis's fights. He returned with yet another knockout story before we had time

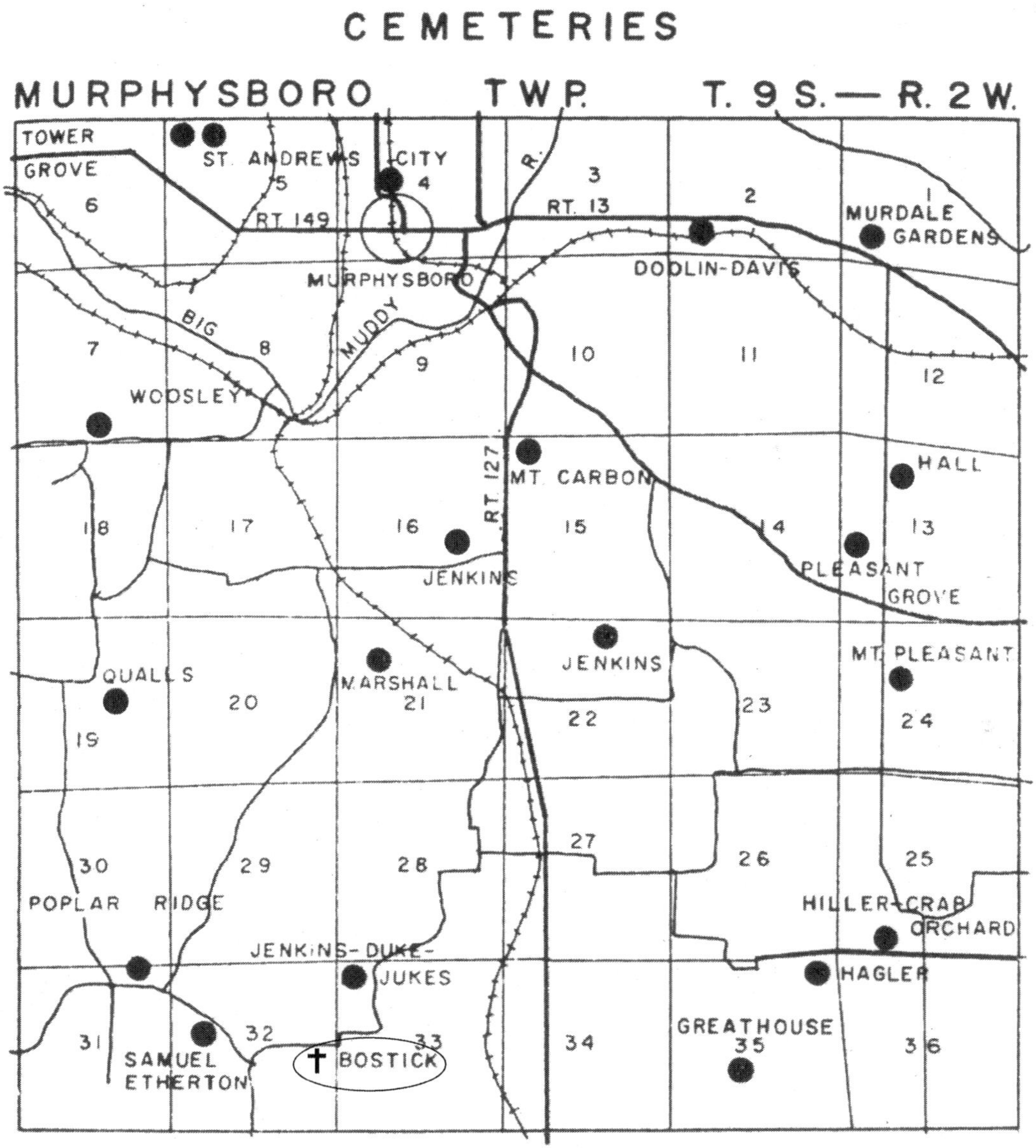

A map showing Bostick Cemetery, established by the Bostick Settlement in the northeast corner of the southeast quarter of section 32, township 9 south, range 2 west of the third principal meridian, Murphysboro Township, Jackson County, Illinois (from *Cemeteries of Jackson County, Illinois, Murphysboro Township*, vol. 5, p. vii, compiled by the Cemetery Committee [W. G. Richison, chairman], Jackson County Historical Society, Murphysboro, 1985).

to miss him. And, of course, Satchel's pitching, Robeson's acting, and Robinson's dancing were the stuff of legends. We had heard of others as well—the movie star Ethel Waters, the singer Marion Anderson, and the scientist George Washington Carver—who were very accomplished people.

I, who grew up with an unquenchable thirst for knowledge of all peoples, could scarcely believe my first encounter with prejudiced people as a young adult. One of the great joys of my life was working at the center of the Southern Illinois University campus at Carbondale, where I could meet and befriend students from any one of the scores of foreign nations represented on campus as a matter of course. And the joys of these encounters only enhanced the memory of the excellent manner in which we children were rooted in kinship with all mankind at a very early age.

Our Old Folks at Home

> All up and down the whole creation,
> Sadly I roam,
> Still longing for the old plantation,
> And for the old folks at home.
>
> —Stephen C. Foster (c. 1850)

With the loss of her mother, a few days after her ninth birthday, always fresh in her memory, Mom determined to fill the void with the cultivation of lasting friendships with a number of memorable ladies in our community.

One of the most memorable was Mrs. Martha Haney at Etherton Switch. Our mother loved Mrs. Haney (I was named after her deceased daughter), and I was impressed with her. At what appeared to me to be a great age, she kept her simple cottage scrupulously clean and grew orderly plots of garden stuffs when she wasn't busy with innumerable other chores. Mrs. Haney was skilled in midwifery and often, on short notice, hitched her horse to the buggy and hurried to the assistance of expectant mothers in the neighborhood. And she often kept the children of those same neighbors while their parents were otherwise occupied. I will never forget the day that I visited her all by myself to take a package from Mom. When I arrived, she was scrubbing clothes on a washboard at the side of the house. She stopped, took me inside, and sat me down at a table covered with a crisp, white tablecloth. She then served a piece of a freshly baked pie that sat in the center of the table. Before I left, she chose several choice items from her garden for me to take back to my mother. I have another enduring memory of Mrs. Haney as a coworker at the Illinois Fruit Growers packing shed at Etherton during the summer of 1938, when I was an impressionable thirteen, and she was a hearty seventy years of age. I watched her quiet diligence that summer with a special interest and marveled at her ability to work the long hours that were sometimes necessary to process a bumper fruit crop.

Martha Falkner Haney, her husband, George, and their baby son, Raymond, in 1888. Martha was born in Mantee, Mississippi, August 19, 1868, to Mr. and Mrs. William Falkner. She and George, a section hand for the Mobile and Ohio Railroad, were married in 1887. The couple established their permanent home in Etherton Switch in Jackson County, Illinois. They were the parents of six children: Raymond T., Bessie, Cleo, Troy, Glenn, and Hamby.

Once in a while Mom would announce an afternoon visit to the home of another memorable lady. We would stroll along a fence row, through a little cottonwood grove, and across a field to see Siota Reeves. She and her husband, Cyrus, lived in a rough-sawn timber house with a metal roof that was nearly as picturesque as our own. Cyrus was a carpenter of the first order. He had built their three-bedroom home entirely of lumber from his own farm. And, long before malls were in style, Cyrus constructed his house and surrounding outbuildings under one extended roof so that one could

Martha and George Haney relaxing at the front stoop of their cottage in Etherton Switch in the mid-1930s. The author and her family, relatives, and friends from near and far attended the Haney's fiftieth wedding anniversary celebration held at their home in 1937. Mr. Haney died in 1945. Grandma Haney, after an almost legendary lifetime of service to her community, died in 1971 at 102 years of age.

go about various chores in inclement weather in perfect comfort. No paint was ever applied to the house, and it weathered to perfection. The house had a lovely foyer and a washroom complete with a washstand and mirror and a towel on a roller. And anyone eating at Siota's table had to be clean and properly clothed, with hair neatly combed, for one didn't say grace in an unkempt condition. Cyrus and Siota had other amenities not common in the area, like a battery-powered radio and a telephone (three shorts and one long was their ring). Cyrus paid for the telephone by walking the country roads after storms to make the necessary line and phone repairs.

Siota Hagler (born February 5, 1870, one of the thirteen children of Matthias and Rebecca McNier Hagler) in a photograph taken in Murphysboro in 1891. Siota's father was a Civil War veteran. Her mother, Rebecca, "came over the water" to become one of the first pioneer ladies of Jackson County, Illinois. In 1917, Siota's son Hiram, who died in 1988 at ninety-two years of age, sailed back across the same water to fight in France with the 26th Yankee Division, Company I, 103rd Infantry, U.S. Army.

I liked looking at all the things in Siota's house, but I never hung around while she and Mother talked because there was an abundance of flowers and herbs outside that had to be scrutinized during the visit. I am sure Mom enjoyed the conversation, though. Siota had some stories to tell: for example, how she had fixed breakfast before dawn in the early years of her marriage, worked in the fields until noon, fixed dinner, and returned to the fields to work until time to fix supper. And how had a turn-of-the-century wife with a new baby handled all of these chores? She took the baby with her, of course. And how had she kept it occupied while she worked? A small dollop of honey on a tiny finger with a feather planted in it kept the baby busy until it fell asleep.

And there was Mrs. Blust. She lived just a few yards down the road from Sharon School. Our family (Mom and Dad, Lester, George, Wayne, and Ethel) had

Siota's tall, handsome beau, Cyrus Reeves (born July 12, 1869, to George and Jane Griffin Reeves), in an 1891 photograph also taken in Murphysboro. Siota (an Indian name) and Cyrus were married October 15, 1891.

Cyrus and Siota Reeves in the flower garden at their home place on the occasion of their fifty-fifth wedding anniversary in 1946. Cyrus and Siota were the parents of seven children—Essie, Hiram, Hommel, Amiel, Bessie, Roy Thomas, and Bert. Amiel and Bessie died as infants, Roy Thomas died of diphtheria as a child, and Hommel died of tuberculosis as a young man. Essie, Hiram, and Bert were blessed with longevity like their parents. Cyrus died July 30, 1959, at ninety years of age. "Aunt Ot," as Siota was affectionately known, died July 30, 1961, two years later to the day, at ninety-one.

lived on the Charlie Blust place just before our home place was purchased in 1924. I remember Mrs. Blust calling on my mother one lovely summer afternoon. They sat in rocking chairs in our sun-splashed living room and talked quietly for hours. Once, Mother asked me to take a package to Mrs. Blust. When school recessed, I carried the bundle proudly down the road to her home, which bordered the school ground. Mrs. Blust invited me into the cool, darkened depths of her elegantly appointed parlor, where a cuckoo clock was cuckooing away the hour. I stood there spellbound while she packaged a return gift for me to carry home to Mom. I could hardly wait. I wanted to talk about the cuckoo clock. And a shiny sofa which, I was amazed to learn, was covered with a horsehair fabric.

Then, of course, there was the Lewis Etherton family from whom Dad had purchased our home place. They lived on the adjoining farm. Our parents considered Lewis and Mary to be their best friends, and there was considerable contact between our two families. The event that stands out in my memory was the occasion of the fiftieth wedding anniversary of Lewis and his wife. What I remember about this occasion is the fact that their granddaughter, Lora Jean, had hair as black as mine but with beautiful curls. I pondered those curls for a long time afterward and determined to learn how to make some of my own.

Lewis and Mary Etherton at their home place with their children—Delia, Elbert, Dolly, Carl, and Ada—and assorted dolls and dogs in 1898. Lewis (born February 14, 1865) and Mary (born December 5, 1868), both of English ancestry, were married August 16, 1885. They lived all their married life in this house, which was built in the early 1870s. In 1948 George Caraway purchased the Etherton house and the 160-acre farm surrounding it and began buying adjoining land as it became available. George died September 7, 2004. Parcels of his land are being acquired by new owners now, but the land he loved and worked for so many years will continue to be an important part of our Caraway family history.

The sea of relatives, friends, and neighbors who came to the Etherton home place to celebrate Lewis and Mary's fiftieth wedding anniversary in the summer of 1935. The author (age ten at the time) and her mother are near the big tree in the upper left corner of the photograph. Lewis and Mary are in the center of the group, behind their anniversary cake. Lewis died October 17, 1939, just four years after this country-style banquet. "Aunt Mary" died February 9, 1963, at ninety-five years of age.

Portraits of Merritt M. Caraway (age twenty-two) and Melvina Powell (age eighteen) copied from tintypes made before their October 20, 1878, wedding in Eldorado, Illinois. (Note the tiara of flowers in Melvina's hair.) Both Merritt and Melvina, the author's paternal grandparents, were born in Wilson County, Tennessee. Their families moved to Saline County, Illinois, during the early months of the Civil War. They were the parents of six children—Bessie and Nellie, who died as infants, Ella, Emma, a stillborn infant daughter who was a twin to Emma, and Charless (the author's father). Melvina died in Jackson County, January 26, 1926, at sixty-five years of age.

Of course, there were memorable gentlemen in our lives, too, the most important one being our own Grandpa Caraway. Our maternal grandparents, Johanna and McFarland Rowan, had died before our parents were married, Johanna after childbirth and McFarland of complications from typhoid fever. And Grandma Melvina Caraway had died when I was one year old. So Grandpa was special, indeed. When he was living with us, as he frequently did in his latter years, I was impressed with his handsome, chiseled face and fine silver hair. But it was his quiet dignity and self-taught knowledge that caused me to hold him, then and now, in certain reverence.

Old "Cap" Wilton was another notable gentleman in our community. He was a man "of considerable means," as my father would say, who lived in the big white farmhouse down the road from the M&O Fruit Farm. Mr. Wilton had a nifty black buggy with a tiny stove in it so he could travel about in total comfort in all kinds of weather. I remember him as a tall, sturdy-looking man, even after he was stricken with cancer (the first time we children had heard anything about this terrible disease). After his death, Mr. Wilton's son, Fred, used his black buggy to deliver the mail on our rural route.

Merritt and Charless Caraway (the author's grandfather and father) at a family gathering at Emma Caraway Hiller's home in 1936. Merritt was a descendant of John Caraway, who was born about 1620 in York County, England. John came to the American colonies in 1644 as an indentured servant and died, about 1669, a landowner in Lower Norfolk County, Virginia. Merritt lived all his adult life on southern Illinois farms and died in Jackson County February 27, 1944, at eighty-seven years of age.

And William Walter Trobaugh, a distinguished-looking gentleman with a gracious demeanor, seemed the epitome of wisdom and goodness to me. He ran a small convenience store on the campus of Southern Illinois Normal University in Carbondale, but we knew him best as the Sunday school superintendent at the Mount Pleasant Methodist Church in Carbondale, which we attended. He served the church, which was built in 1869 on land donated by his father, in this capacity from 1908 to 1968. His imposing presence in our house of worship all those years ago lent a never-to-be-forgotten quality to Sunday mornings.

Occasionally, we traveled about to visit special people. Mother never made a trip to the Rowan Cemetery at Makanda to tend her parents' graves without stopping for a visit in the home of Ida Mae Lirely. Before her marriage, Mom had sometimes cared for the younger Lirely children, and the bond of friendship between the two women was never broken. I have one particularly poignant memory in connection with this family that Mother would have loved. One of Ida Mae's seven sons, the Reverend William H. Lirely, at memorial services for Dad in 1977, remembered his own childhood days when the beautiful Bessie Mae cared for him and the day "when a handsome young man came across the field" to take his "sweetheart" away.

These few old folks were special to all of us, but there were others, as well, who have permanent places in our memories.

William Walter Trobaugh in his small general store, which he operated at several locations on the Southern Illinois University campus from 1932 to 1972. (This location was just north of where the Student Center now stands.) Born on a large farm in Murphysboro Township in 1879, Trobaugh first came to Southern Illinois Normal University as a student in 1898, when the campus consisted of Main and Altgeld Halls. He attended SINU for two years, then spent some years as a school teacher and farmer before opening his campus business. He retired from the landmark store at the age of ninety-two and died at ninety-seven in Carbondale.

Ida Mae Elliott, born June 28, 1874, one of five children of George and Sarah Elliott of Makanda, Illinois. Ida Mae was sixteen when this photograph was made. Her parents had just been told by the family physician that she might have tuberculosis. Thinking that Ida Mae's death was imminent, they decided to have a formal portrait of her made at the Normal Art Gallery in Carbondale. Ida Mae boiled quince seed to make a solution for her hair and rolled it up in rags to achieve the glossy curls shown in the photograph.

Ida Mae Elliott Lirely, her husband Charles Jacob, and their nine children in August 20, 1932, at the family farm near Makanda, Illinois, on the occasion of Jacob's birthday. Shown in the front row (*left to right*) are Eula Anita, Charles Jacob, Ida Mae, and Fannie Alice. In the back row are Robert Elliott, George Allen, Oscar Wesley, Ivan Berthold, William Herbert, Samuel Albert, and Charles Millard. The couple lived all their married life on this farm. Jacob, a descendant of a seventeenth-century immigrant to the American colonies from the region of Lake Constance on the German-Swiss border, died on May 12, 1938, at seventy years of age. "Grannie Mae" died July 12, 1944, also at seventy years of age.

In the Evening by the Lamplight

Do folks today enjoy their evenings out, or in, as much as we did? I doubt it.

There were always books to read. Mom and Dad had collected some paperbacks and a few classics that were read and reread and placed back on the shelf to be read again. The books were kept on the tall side of the bookcase-commode. The lower side had a shelf for a wash basin and pitcher with a cupboard underneath for a chamber pot (all the amenities, in one compact design, a person could ask for on a cold winter night).

Then there were the nights when Charlie and Coy Ellis (the grown-up sons of our neighbors who had moved onto the Ott Modglin place) came over with guitar, harmonica, and Jew's harp to make our rafters ring. We loved it!

To the north, for a while, our neighbors were the Bill Etherton family. Bill was a real cowboy. When he and his three daughters came to see us, we listened to true-to-life tales of the "wild west."

And, when Grandpa Caraway was staying with us, he would tell us, at our urging, ghost stories which made our hair stand on end and stay that way long after we'd gone to bed.

I have no clear memory of the rather elegant little organ that once graced our home, but George remembers the day Mom purchased it from Aunt Sally Greathouse and had it removed from her cabin to our place. Nor do I remember that Mom worked diligently at the keyboard to train herself to play by ear, since there was no one in our immediate vicinity to teach her properly. I find it infinitely pleasant, though, to reflect on this facet of my mother's character that required her to use every opportunity to improve herself or to make her surroundings more pleasant. The sad part of this story is that I do remember how we children soon destroyed her organ (one of us would manipulate the foot pedals while another pressed the keys).

Always on the lookout for bargains that would enrich our lives, Mom came home from town one day with a Victrola with a hand crank, dozens of records,

Logan and Ada Viola Garris Ellis in the mid-1940s, when the family lived in Carbondale. Logan, born August 3, 1881, in a community called Boyleston, near Fairfield, Illinois, was part Choctaw Indian. Ada, born September 22, 1892, in a community near Dogwood Mines in Jackson County, Illinois, was one-half Cherokee (her father was a full-blooded Cherokee). Married in Williamson County in 1907, they were the parents of nine children: Roy, Vivian, Charles, Evelyn, Coy, Eugene, Victor, Barbara, and Zella. The four younger children went to Sharon School in the early 1930s when the family lived on the Lon Hagler place to the north and then the Modglin place just south of the author's home. Logan, a farmer and a miner most of his life, was employed during the depths of the Depression in Roosevelt's Work Projects Administration program and died in 1955 at seventy-four years of age. Ada, nicknamed "Hanner" by friends and neighbors, was seventy-nine when she died in 1971. Their son Charles, blinded in a sawmill accident in 1941, was southern Illinois' famed caner craftsman and an ordained minister of the Gospel. He died December 26, 1991, at seventy-eight years of age. The author remembers young Charlie and Coy as the big boys who accompanied the smaller children to school on snowy days to lift them over drifts, and as the makers of music at family gatherings on winter nights and summer Sundays.

and a box of extra needles. We were ecstatic. A few of the records have stuck in my mind, like "The Old Chisholm Trail," "Springtime in the Rockies," "Big Rock Candy Mountain," "Paper of Pins," and "The Preacher and the Bear." In the last, the preacher had climbed a persimmon tree to escape a bear in hot pursuit. We would go into spasms of laughter each time we heard the words:

"Oh Lord, didn't you deliver Daniel from the lion's den?
Also deliver Jonah from the belly of the whale and then,
three Hebrew children from the fiery furnace
so the good books do declare,
Now Lord if you can't help me
for goodness sake, don't you help that bear."

Sometime after that, Mom brought home a radio. Not just a radio. This was a beautiful radio with a tall matching cabinet. Thereafter, we hurried through supper to retire to the living room. Prickles of excitement ran over me as Walter Winchell bade us a "Good evening, Mr. and Mrs. North and South America and all the ships at sea." Or, there was Gabriel Heatter with his "Ah, there's good news tonight." And then came the mysteries and the serials. And music from WLS Chicago with our favorites, Lulu Belle and Scotty. And Amos and Andy. And the Lone Ranger.

There were also hard-fought games of dominoes and jacks. And the cracking of our own walnuts or the shelling of homegrown peanuts roasted in our own oven. And a game called the Cat's Cradle in which a string is looped in a pattern like a cradle on the fingers of one child's hand and transferred to the hands of another so as to form a different figure. And a lot of shadow painting on the wall in the glow of the kerosene lamp.

If we were lucky enough to be snowbound, as in Whittier's poem, Mom would stir up a great batch of snow ice cream (a mixture of snow "untouched by human hands," cream, sugar, and vanilla extract). The luxury of a bowl of delicately flavored frozen ice crystals, no two of which were ever alike, was something to be savored!

When Dad rose to bank the fires of our coal-burning heating stove, it was time to go to bed.

> Within our beds awhile we heard
> The wind that round the gables roared,
> With now and then a ruder shock,
> Which made our very bedsteads rock.
> We heard the loosened clapboards tost,
> The board-nails snapping in the frost;
> And on us, through the unplastered wall,
> Felt the light sifted snow-flakes fall.
> But sleep stole on, as sleep will do
> When hearts are light and life is new;
> Faint and more faint the murmurs grew,
> Till in the summer-land of dreams
> They softened to the sound of streams,
> Low stir of leaves, and dip of oars,
> And lapsing waves on quiet shores.
>
> —John Greenleaf Whittier, *Snowbound*

Part Three ❧ Shangri-la

Wait Till Our Cows Come Home

In the early years after Dad purchased the home place in 1924, he built up quite a herd of milk cows. At four o'clock each morning, he and the boys (Lester and George) headed for the barn to do the milking. And, of course, the process was repeated in the evenings. Sometimes we younger children had to herd the cows back home in the evenings if they seemed to be tarrying too long in the pasture.

As I remember our dairy operation, Mom's job (with our assistance) was to wash the buckets the milkers used and the component parts of the cream separator, along with the milk and cream cans for the excess milk and cream we sold. And putting the separator back together was an engineering feat not to be lightly attempted—if it wasn't assembled properly, it didn't work!

For many years, we had milk products for sale. Early in our operation, our cream was collected in containers in our cool earthen cellar beneath the house (in really hot weather we hung it in the well) and sold weekly to C. Silvey's Creamery in Murphysboro. Sometimes we shipped it in to them by train from Etherton Switch. Later we sold whole milk, which was picked up by Bill Sauer each morning. Finally, a large truck came from the New Era Dairy in Carbondale to pick up our milk daily.

But we didn't sell all our milk. We kept back enough for our daily use on hot cereal and in coffee at breakfast and to drink morning and evening. We used sweet milk for cooking and clabber milk for biscuits. Occasionally, we churned whole milk for butter and the by-product, buttermilk. Sometimes, Mother made a superb cottage cheese. Our cats always got generous helpings, and the hogs got any surplus. Nothing was wasted.

We children loved our cows and often went to the barn lot just to watch them chew their cuds. Once in a while, something really exciting happened in our barn. Like the morning Mother awakened us with the news that we had twin calves. Of course, we all had to tromp down to the barn to see them before we went to school. And one day, when Dad was working a field at the back of the farm and Lester and George were at the M&O, one of our cows chose to have her calf at the far end of the pasture in a cottonwood grove. Mom suspected that something like that was happening, and we went looking for them. Mom carried that newborn calf all the way back to the barn, stopping ever so often to rest. I remember thinking that the calf was too heavy for her, but she was determined to get it home safe and sound. And she did. Even now, I have a vivid image of Mother fetching that calf with a somewhat resentful cow following in her wake.

An occasional shipment to market was something our parents banked on but not something to be taken lightly. I mean those cows lived just across the fence and could actually reach their long necks over, under, or through the fence to munch grass right from our yard. So we got to know them personally and missed them when they were gone.

When our cows went dry, we made do. I recall the perfectly awful oleo margarine with the little packets of coloring that had to be mixed in, if it was humanly possible to get a mix. It was a pale, pale imitation of the real thing! This notwithstanding, our farm seemed to us like Shangri-la, the hilly utopia of James Hilton's 1933 best-selling novel *Lost Horizon.*

Here Chickens, There Chickens

My mother, ingenious in ways to make extra money and feed her brood simultaneously, ordered a kerosene-heated incubator (for a small down payment and so much a week) in which she intended to hatch chicks. She was so successful at her little enterprise that she staffed our chicken house and hatched chickens for our neighbors as well. There were several intriguing facets to this operation. One was the fact that Mom could determine by means of a makeshift x-ray (a rolled-up newspaper and a flashlight) that certain eggs were infertile. Another was the hatching process itself. The incubator had see-through front doors, which were manned tirelessly by us children when the magic birthing was taking place. Big Bird of *Sesame Street* will never have the rapt attention we gave those chicklets as they pecked their way to freedom in that incubator.

Before Mom got her incubator, she had to order her baby chickens from a hatchery. Our mailbox was situated on our lane in the hollow between the house and the garden. When Mr. Boucher sailed right by the box, we knew he had something special for us. In the early spring, it was likely a perforated box filled to overflowing with baby chicks. What a racket those tiny balls of yellow fuzz could make! I couldn't imagine how Mr. Boucher could stand it all the way from town!

The chickens had a very fine house complete with a wood-burning stove to keep them warm in the chill spring weather, but sometimes Mother took them right into the kitchen in a space behind the stove for a while so she could watch them carefully. If there were any sickly ones, she tended them until they were better. The nurturing of our chickens was a big job. They had to have corn, laying mash, oyster shells, water twice daily, and just about anything else their craws might desire. These chickens were meat for our table. And they laid eggs, lots of eggs for us to eat or sell in town. Mother's egg money was the source of any "extras" that we came by for many years. So if she lost even one chicken, it was a serious blow.

When the young chickens were big enough to walk through grass without falling over, we gave them the run of the hillside back of the chicken house. And they seemed to prosper in their freedom. There were problems, though. At the base of the hill, a stream meandered along on its way to Sugar Creek. In a heavy rain, the stream rose over its banks. So when rain threatened, we had our work cut out for us. The object was to get the strays on the wrong side of the creek back up the hill, but the chickens simply didn't want to go in *until* it started raining. It always seemed to me on these occasions that my chickens eluded me with great skill, while the ones my mother went after fairly leapt into her outstretched apron. Anyway, after one of these roundups, we all (Mom, the chickens, and the children) were a bedraggled mess. But we soon dried out.

Occasionally, one of these chickens really got under your skin. I had one little pet who would run smack into my arms and cuddle in my lap like a kitten. I was devastated when my pet sickened and died. I think the awful truth is that I fed it too much dry cornbread one day.

And on Our Farm There Was a Pig

I was, more or less, a loner during that period when my baby brother, Charley, was too little to play with me and I was too young to go to school. Dad and Mom were well aware of my situation and went to some lengths to provide interesting activities. On one occasion, my mother suggested that I help Dad feed the hogs. He agreed, and in addition to the ten-gallon bucket of mash he would carry, he mixed a one-gallon bucket for me. We walked side by side down the driveway to the lane that led to our hog pen some distance from our house. I was fairly strutting—it was great!

When we arrived at the pen, Dad opened the gate and stepped inside the fence. I followed. Without any warning, one of the piglets charged me. I did what any sensible person would do: I defended myself. My bucket of mash connected with the pig's head, and he fell dead.

Dad, after verification of my deed, grabbed a large butcher knife that he kept at the site, slit the pig's throat, and hung him by his feet on the fence. I, completely stunned by the turn of events, watched anxiously as he calmly went about the feeding routine.

Back at the house, we had a newly butchered pig to process. My father, of course, did the cleaning and cutup, and my mother launched into a cooking and canning routine (we had no refrigeration then) that lasted well into the night. The pig was small, but the by-products of the slaying filled many containers, all of which were promptly stored in the cellar under the house.

My mother probably could have done without my presence, but I waited in the backyard near the kitchen door and sent her vibes of my abject misery all the while. When she had finished dealing with this unexpected slaughter on our country lane, she tucked me into bed for a sleepless night.

Fortunately, the memories of legitimate slaughtering operations on our farm are so vivid that I can almost forget that earlier mishap. To begin with, we stayed home from school for a butchering. Even with a neighbor's assistance, which was usual, all available hands were needed. After the actual slaughtering, which I never witnessed, came the scalding, scraping, and cutup. Then there was fat to be trimmed from the entrails, scrap meat to be ground, a fire to be maintained under the huge iron cauldron in the backyard where the fat was rendered into lard, and errands to be run between the slaughtering site and the house. Some of the meat was cured with salt. The hams were smoked in a specially constructed, vented earthen chamber. Mother seasoned the ground meat with her magic blend of herbs and spices and began immediately to cook down and can the sausages. Then, of course, there was head cheese to be made, feet to be pickled, and mincemeat to be prepared for pies. Again, nothing was wasted.

The prize for this day of strenuous activity was a supper of prime tenderloin prepared to perfection. The taste and smell still linger in my memory. Of course, some prime cuts were sent home with any neighbor who assisted because the courtesy would be returned when Dad helped elsewhere. And, finally, there were generous helpings of cracklings, a residue delicacy created from the rendering process, which we enjoyed around the evening fire.

For the most part, these butcherings were not affairs to be taken to heart. The hogs lived way down the road from the house, and we weren't that friendly with them. But there was one who was born a runt and bound to change things. Actually, he grew up in the backyard and came to think of himself as the family dog. I can't remember what happened to him, though, and I am afraid to ask someone who would know.

A Child's Best Friend

We had a yard full of company that summer Sunday. Several cars lined the circle drive. Charley had climbed onto the running board of one of the cars. Suddenly, the car started rolling down the drive. Fritz grabbed him by the seat of his rompers and pulled him free of the moving car as if he did that sort of thing daily. George stopped the car before it rolled off down the hill, and another disaster had been avoided.

But it wasn't the occasional deeds of derring-do that won Fritz a permanent place in our hearts. It was the day-to-day comradeship, the sure knowledge that he was our friend. He came to us as a fuzzy little fellow barely out of the weaning stage. He was dumped at our door, or near enough that he found his way to us, and he stayed.

Fritz's hunting skills were well known. And if our feathered friends, wildlings or otherwise, lived an erstwhile existence around our home place, the ones with fur were in real jeopardy. Because Lester and George, at a young age, but ably assisted by Fritz, were hunters and trappers of the first order. There was a ready market for furs (mink, fox, raccoon, et cetera) in Chicago. The boys ran their winter traplines in the frigid morning hours before dawn and then skinned their animals and tacked the skins to boards to make them ready for shipping. But the trips over field and stream that the threesome made for the express purpose of bringing back food for our table are most prominent in my memory. I can see the boys coming in with the large rabbits swinging from their belts as they walked and Fritz as obviously satisfied as a good hunting dog can be without being cocky about it.

By the time I was twelve years old, Fritz had aged and sickened nigh unto death. The decision was made that he had to be destroyed. As Dad led him down to the pasture with gun in hand, several of us children formed an impromptu support circle in the backyard and clung to one another as we waited for the crack of the rifle. And when we heard it, we cried as if we had lost a dear brother.

Dad told me years later that he neither slept nor ate for two days afterward. The truth is that Fritz, like no other animal, played a major role in our lives at the home place. Sometime back, when I was thinking along these same lines, I wrote a tribute of my own:

Ol' Fritz

We were a family of nine on a farm
and, at one time or another, had such rich and rare things
as a "copper-bottom" horse named Ol' Dan
and a billy goat
and "runt" pigs with ringlet tails
and downy, yellow chicks
and gentle cows with wobbly-legged, newborn calves
and soft, furry kittens;
but Ol' Fritz—he was one of us.

On bright spring days
he lay quietly with us in dewy meadows of sweet clover
as we sipped nectar from the blossoms
and traced funny faces in the fleecy clouds.

He walked the dusty country roads with us
barefoot in the summer heat;
and in the cool, twilight hours under the big yard trees
he raced the wind with us
until we fell exhausted on the green carpets of grass.

In the winter he tramped with the boys through snowy fields
to bring back rabbits and other game for the table;
and he tarried, warm and contented, in the kitchen
while our mother prepared the succulent dishes.

He was the essence of tranquility;
but if our leaf-canopied lane yielded strangers,
he became the fierce family protector.

Always he kept watch over us
as we indulged in forbidden childhood delights
like swimming in rain-swollen creeks after sudden summer storms
or wandering in the wooded areas far too far from home.

He was our playmate, our guardian.
We claimed his love and devotion,
and he knew we returned it in equal measure.
Many years have passed since the day he left us,
blind and weak from age,
but it seems like yesterday . . .
Love encompasses time.

Pussy Cat, Pussy Cat

In *Foothold on a Hillside*, my father told a cat tale about Wampus, who was, as he said, "one helluva cat." There were others on our farm from time to time, of course.

One memorable tabby cat comes to mind. She had just given birth to six kittens and was so proud she could barely stand it, coming to the house often to get somebody to come and look at them. She had chosen the unused room of the chicken house as her birthing place. One morning we heard a terrible, mournful cry. When we investigated, we found that each kitten had been bitten through the neck and laid out in a neat row. The mother was walking back and forth, back and forth, crying loudly all the while. Lester and George loaded up their rifles and, with Ol' Fritz leading the way, headed for the woods. Just down the hill, Ol' Fritz treed a giant woods cat. The boys shot the cat dead and brought him back for us to see. But our mother cat was inconsolable and literally died of grief. We came close.

We had another unforgettable cat. Aunt Ella and Uncle Arthur (Dad's sister and her husband) came over one day. They liked one of our cats very much and were given permission to take her home with them. She didn't want to go, of course. Dad had to put her in a tow sack to stop her resistance (he would never have done so had he not known that our cat would have a royal existence at the end of the ride). A few days later, the cat showed up, hungry and ragged, at the doorstep. Needless to say, she was never sent away again.

Our place was truly a haven for cats. I can still see all our cats in a row in the back yard, paws perfectly placed, waiting for Dad to come up from the barn with a bucket of warm milk just for them.

Betty and one of the Caraway cats.

To Market, to Market

Occasionally, Mother bought condiments and the like from a well-stocked traveling Jewel Tea Company truck or a Raleigh salesman, but that was rare. And going to town for staples—Gold Medal all-purpose flour, Clabber Girl baking powder, Arm & Hammer baking soda, Quaker rolled oats, Sun Maid raisins, rice, coffee, cocoa, sugar, salt, black pepper, spices, yeast, and vinegar—could turn out to be a very interesting affair.

Our first stop was A&P No. 1 grocery store run by Harry Sangwin. Mother always had a large bucket of fresh eggs to trade. Mr. Sangwin counted those eggs with almost sleight-of-hand rapidity and kept the aggregate total in his head. There was always the almost breathless expectation that an egg would slip out of his grasp and splatter on the smooth countertop, but it never happened. I often think now, after a frantic trip through a supermarket, that we've regressed in the business of grocerying. With her list firmly in hand, my mother never moved from her place at the counter. Mr. Sangwin didn't have to move far either. The store was just about as high as it was wide, and he used a pole with an attached hook to expertly pull items from the top shelves into his waiting hands. Again, he never missed. And the beauty of it all was that the egg money covered, or came close to covering, the cost of our staples.

Our next stop was sometimes J. C. Penney's dry goods store on Walnut Street. We children always made a beeline for the large scale that guarded the entrance to this store for one reason—it told your fortune while it weighed you. Penney's had ready-to-wear, but Mother generally shopped there for yard goods, buttons, rickrack and lace, elastic, patterns, and the like. Watching a clerk slap a large bolt of cloth on the countertop and measure off the proper yardage was fascinating stuff. There was a big box of remnants at the end of the counter that Mother kept her eye on, too. Dad had a cobbler's last and supplies for repairing shoes, but we usually had to visit Penney's shoe department once a year for new back-to-school wear (shoes and buckle overshoes). The problem of coaxing feet that had gone bare all summer long into new shoes was eased somewhat by the prospect of peering through Penney's magic fluoroscope to see if toes had room to grow in shoes that might be purchased. And, best of all, when a sale was consummated, you could watch the sales slip and an accompanying bill go by a little trolley from floor level to an upstairs cage where change was made and sent flying back down in nothing flat!

Once in a while we visited other clothing stores in Murphysboro, too. If Mother needed ready-to-wear for the men and boys in her family that she couldn't find at Penney's, we shopped at the Square Deal Clothing House. And, in the less likely event that she wanted to buy a ready-made garment for herself or her girls, we visited Ross's Store. My first store-bought dress came from Ross's and was purchased for my graduation from the eighth grade at Sharon School. It was an elegant green crepe princess line with a white lace collar. After this purchase, we went back to Penney's to buy my first pair of "high-heeled" pumps and my first pair of silk hose (nylon hose were not marketed until 1939).

The J. C. Penney Company store at 1324 Walnut Street in Murphysboro, 1926. Note the straw boaters, sturdy shoes, umbrellas, ready-to-wear, and yard goods all charmingly displayed in the store windows. In 1971 this small store in Murphysboro, where the author and her family shopped in the 1930s, was closed when the company opened a new store at the University Mall in Carbondale.

The Square Deal Clothing House in its original location, across from the courthouse in Murphysboro during the late 1930s. David Baer, who founded the store at 1008 Walnut Street in 1887, left the Alsace province in northeastern France in 1871, when the region was invaded by Chancellor Bismarck's armies, and came to New York City, where he learned English and worked for a time at various jobs. He ended up working in a clothing store owned by A. Lederer in DeSoto, Missouri. They opened a store in Murphysboro later, and Baer bought Lederer out in 1887. Joseph Baer, David's son, took over the store when David died in 1923 at sixty-three years of age. Burke Yeager, who became a Square Deal employee at age sixteen after both his parents died, and Edward Althoff bought the store from Joseph in 1953. Burke soon became the sole owner of the store and remained so until he died January 31, 1992, at eighty-five years of age. On October 1, 1992, the Square Deal Clothing House moved lock, stock, and barrel to 801 Walnut Street, where it remained until recently. In June 2006 the present owners, Phyllis Yeager Grob and her daughter Carolyn Gallegly, bought their own building and moved the landmark family business with all its original antique furnishings to 1607 Walnut Street.

Ross's Store at 1218 Walnut Street in Murphysboro (circa mid-1930s). The owner, Samuel Ross, was born in Alexandria in the then Russian Ukraine in 1886, where his father was foreman of the nearby estate of the great writer Count Lev Nikolayevich Tolstoy. Ross, a Jew, escaped the pogrom in Russia by enlisting in the army and then leaving, hiding during the day and walking under cover of darkness across the frontier into Austria with a friend. Sam then made his way across Europe and embarked for the United States, arriving in Boston January 16, 1907. After staying there for a time, he went to St. Louis to take over the peddling route of an uncle who wished to return to Alexandria. Traveling the countryside by horse and buggy to sell fabric and household goods over a number of years, Ross earned enough money to bring all the remaining members of his family out of Russia. In 1920 Sam and his brother, Solomon, started a skirt manufacturing business in a loft in St. Louis and then bought William Roth's clothing store in Murphysboro, Illinois, moving there in 1922. In the next few years, Sam, Sol, and their brother, Sidney, opened stores in Du Quoin and Carbondale, Illinois, and in Cape Girardeau, Missouri. In 1950 Sam became the sole owner of the Murphysboro store. Sam's wife, Fanny, died in 1939, but Sam remained active in community affairs well into his eighties and died in 1982 at ninety-six years of age. Sam and Fanny had two daughters, Esther and RoseLee. Esther (a high school classmate of the author) and her husband, Sydney Appleton, owned Ross's of Murphysboro until the store closed in 1994 after seventy-two years in business.

F. W. Woolworth's was a likely stop, too. While Mother shopped there, I liked to walk on down the aisle just to hear the sound of the squeaking wooden floors. At the back of this store, you could sometimes see a platform elevator take on merchandise from a conveyance at street level and lift it upstairs to be stored until ready for sale. An even better place to congregate in the summertime was the front of the store, where generous ice cream cones and sandwiches were sold out of a portable stand. Another option was a hole-in-the-wall shop right down the street that sold ice-cold draft root beer in big, frosty mugs for five cents.

I mean, you simply couldn't lose! Of course, if we did take on refreshments at either place, the next stop was the courthouse, with its cool marble halls and graffiti-covered restroom walls. Mother never let us tarry there, and certain questions went unanswered or were never asked.

And, if we had time and a few pennies that were burning holes in our pockets, Mother would take us to the post office to buy postal savings stamps.

We never asked to go to town, though. And, when we stayed home, there were countless things to do.

In the winter months, the kitchen was always a good place to start. Wayne decided once, and only once, to make us some biscuits. He probably had all the necessary ingredients but not in proper proportion. Judging from the size and texture (they were outsized and hard as rocks), I would say he overdid the baking powder and flour by a long shot.

Another time, Wayne decided to save Mom the trouble of washing his clothes by doing his own laundry. A tub was placed on the stove and water added. When it was hot enough, he poured in some Oxydol. As the flakes dissolved and danced across the surface of the hot water, Wayne exclaimed, "Look at those little Oxy-dolls!" I can only say that the length of time this home-grown witticism has been remembered is the clue to how impressed we were with it.

Popcorn balls were one of our favorite treats, and Mom could make them to perfection. The one time we tried this, the hot molasses stuck to the palm of

Ethel's hand and burned her badly. Mom came home to find her screaming in pain, with pieces of popcorn and molasses still clinging to her blistered palm.

A taffy pull usually generated into a dangerous affair, too, with flour and molasses "from here to kingdom come," as Mother would say, but we gave it a try now and then.

There were other areas of interest, too. Dad had a tobacco caddy in which he kept chewing tobacco, cigars, and the makings for roll-your-own cigarettes. One fateful day, we all sampled his wares and barely lived to tell it. But tell it, we did. There was no punishment other than what we ourselves had devised.

And were there no adults around when we children were cooking up our various projects? Sometimes Grandpa was there in his easy chair in the corner of the living room in the winter or in a lawn chair in the summer. Sleeping, likely, and not to be disturbed. And sometimes we were there alone and charged with responsible conduct. For the most part, we delivered.

Bringing in Our Sheaves

I am sure you have heard about threshing dinners. Now, there was an occasion! Farmers and their wives from around the community gathered to harvest a crop in one fell swoop. The day Mr. Ross's great, lumbering threshing machine made its way to our farm, through cut fences, and over hill and dale to the mature fields was one we met with a barely harnessed excitement. And the food! I've heard it said that too many cooks spoil the pot. Not so. And, besides, when you're feeding a dozen hungry men, with their attendant women and children, you need some extra hands. Both tables in our kitchen and dining room were extended full-length and every available chair and bench (and sometimes wooden crates) were employed to handle the partakers in shifts. And when the day was done, the crops (oats, cowpeas, and Great Northern beans for our table) were in. And the threshing machine lumbered away to the next farm.

But, generally, we did our own harvesting. I well remember one such occasion. I can't remember why the big rush, though. My guess is that the hay was down and the weather was threatening. At any rate, the crop had to be harvested at once. All hands on the farm—men, women, and children—were assigned to the task. Now, hay is baled in the fields before it is brought to the barn. Then, ours was carefully layered on our wagon until it reached a width and height that seemed utterly precarious. It seemed so, but I can't ever remember seeing one of these great, clumsy loads of hay slide off the wagon. Most of the hay made it into the barnyard every time and was then transferred by pitchfork from wagon to barn through a large aperture in the loft. During this particular harvest, I was given the job of taking up the hay that fell to the ground as it was thrown from wagon to loft. As I went about my hot, sticky (but sweet-smelling) task, something glistened in the sun. It was a needle!

> As well look for a needle in a bottle [bundle] of hay.
>
> —Cervantes, *Don Quixote*

Our Green, Green Grass of Home

> 'Mid pleasures and palaces though we may roam,
> Be it ever so humble, there's no place like home.
>
> —John Howard Payne, *Home Sweet Home*

The buildings at the home place Dad and Mom purchased in 1924 were not that great. But Mom immediately set about the business of making our yard so verdant and colorful that the rugged old buildings (the house, smokehouse, chicken house, garage, and privy) would impart a picturesque beauty of their own. And she succeeded.

Our house, in those early years, had a rough-sawn, diagonally mounted timber siding. With years of weathering, the boards had taken on a mossy sheen that seemed very attractive to us children. In the springtime, Mother would make

A 1929 McCormick-Deering tractor (with a thresher of equal vintage) being "driven" by Jean Caraway (George's wife) at their farm. This equipment, owned by Joe VanCloostere, was one of the last of the old-time rigs that traveled about to area farms to process various crops.

a twine latticework from floor to roof of the front porch and train honeysuckle up the strands until the porch area became a shaded and fragrant honeysuckle bower. Inside the bower looking out, we could watch the hummingbirds who visited our honeysuckle vines. We were fascinated that these birds could beat their wings so fast you couldn't see them do it as they flew forward and backward and hovered in the air. And we marveled that this smallest of all birds was the only bird in the whole world who could do these things.

The front porch looked out on a great elm, as well as the eight soft maples that Dad and the boys had brought up from Cedar Creek. Rows of Easter lilies and hyacinths and irises marched along the driveway. Flowering shrubs, like the hydrangea with its huge snowball blossoms, were everywhere. In the back there were red and black cherry trees, a pear tree, plum trees with a sweet pungence that fills my nostrils even now, and a grape arbor on which we learned to skin the cat (a backwards somersault through your arms). But most magnificent of all were the roses of every hue and kind, from pale pink baby dolls to huge velvety maroons, that surrounded the house and lined the adjoining pasture fences. To this day, I find that all other flowers pale in comparison!

As we children became familiar with the abundance of cultivated plants at our home site, we developed a keen fascination with the language of flowers and an inclination toward a corruption of that language. Not a corruption, exactly—more of an inspired alteration to suit one's fancy. The huge elm in our front yard, for instance, became "the big elem." The two syllables seemed more fitting somehow—the tree deserved a special moniker. Its spreading branches provided a cool canopy for us to play under all summer long. Each spring the green grass that sprouted around its trunk was soon worn down by the patter of numerous bare feet. By midsummer the floor of our playhouse was so smooth that we swept it as part of our weekly spiffing up process for Sunday guests.

There were some plants like the sweet pea and the sweet william whose endearing names won our hearts forever. And those with terribly dramatic names like the bleeding heart and love lies bleeding. And some that sent us into spasms of giggles, like our so-called "daffy-dils," the "nasty-turtiums" that our mother always grew, and the "snappy-dragons" with mouths that opened and closed with a slight pressure.

And there were some plants that did very interesting things on their own. Like the tall hollyhocks whose bright faces followed the sun all the day. And the four-o'clocks with fragrant red, yellow, and white flowers that opened late in the afternoon. Mother would send us out when it was nearing time for this marvelous occurrence. But we usually soon forgot our mission and wandered off, only to find the blossoms already opened when we returned.

Many happy hours were spent at play in our yard. Sometimes, of course, we had to be urged into it. Once when we were underfoot in the kitchen, Mother gave us a salt shaker and told us, conspiratorially, that if we sprinkled some salt on the birds' tails they would let us touch them. She had our attention immediately. In school we had learned to recite William Cullen Bryant's poem about the "bob-a-link" with great relish:

> Merrily swinging on briar and weed,
> Near to the nest of his little dame,
> Over the mountain-side or mead,
> Robert of Lincoln is telling his name:
> Bob-a-link, bob-a-link
> Spink, spank, spink; . . .

So, when Mother stilled us on occasion and pointed out that some birds, like the mockingbird, the whip-poor-will, and the bobwhite, could talk quite well, we listened attentively and marveled at these creatures.

There was also a fascination with the wonders of mud. Under "the big elem" we mixed the clay from roadsides with a few dippers of water and made perfectly executed fruit (usually gooseberry) pies. Crusts were rolled out with bottle rolling pins, perforated with old case knives, and fluted around the edges just like Mom's. One morning Wayne built a life-size tricycle that looked real enough to ride. When we came back after our dinner break, it had dried out and fallen apart. Wayne strove valiantly to keep from crying, but he simply couldn't handle the loss.

We often spent not only our daylight hours in the yard but also our twilight hours as well, chasing the magic fireflies to and fro. But they, like the birds, were very elusive.

One patch in the backyard where we hopscotched regularly was worn smooth, but the rest of the yard had to have some maintenance. For a while, we had a built-in lawn mower named Billy (our pet billy goat). All we had to do was stake him out, and he did the rest. Later, when Billy was no longer with us, Dad or Lester or George would take the scythe to the tall grass first (the scythe was not an instrument to be wielded by the unskilled, and I remember thinking what a marvelously rhythmic task it was as performed by the men in our family). Then we children did the close work with the hand sickle. I have a suspicion that our yard never looked manicured, but I recall being very pleased with the finished product after our periodic cleanup campaigns.

One spring Dad brought up a load of flat rocks from the creek bed, and Mom constructed a circular rock garden in which she planted brilliantly blooming rose moss for another bright spot in our lives.

And from our yard there was the vista, a panoramic view of rolling green hills and vales dotted with grazing cattle and horses. It may not have seemed so to others, but we thought springtime in our own Shangri-la in the foothills of the Illinois Ozarks lovely, indeed!

We Came to the Garden Alone

Now that I think of it, it must have been by design that there was a lovely patch of lane between our house and our garden. It was always such an occasion to go to "The Garden," even if you did it twice a day. As we traipsed to and fro, we formed regular little processions with Mom leading the way and children bringing up the rear.

Dad broke the ground in the ridge-top plot for Mom each spring, and she took it from there. We children were allowed to help with some of the hoeing, raking, weeding, and, eventually, harvesting. Pests were usually dealt with individually, and Mom had some expert help in that department. She found Charley's romper pockets full of tomato worms at the end of one day when he had patiently shadowed her down the long garden rows.

The physical layout of the garden was almost sculptured. A grape arbor extended along one end of the plot. There were lettuce and spinach beds. And rows of tomatoes, onions, peppers, radishes, cabbages, cucumbers, carrots, and beets. And sage and dill beds. And gooseberry, blackberry, and raspberry bushes. And a strawberry patch. And beyond this prime plot, there were others where watermelons and cantaloupes, Irish and sweet potatoes, sweet corn, green beans, peas, and cane were grown in quantity. It took a lot of these staples to feed seven children, their parents, and a grandparent.

Harvesting came early sometimes. Like our secretive trips to the strawberry patch while the dew was still on the roses to pluck the first of the season. Usually, Mom would not let on. And, occasionally, she would deliver freshly baked rolls to our "playhouse" (a motley collection of rough planks assembled by Wayne that made the Our Gang clubhouse look like a small mansion), where we took our stolen delights.

The real harvests were just as much fun, with all hands on deck. And, when our table was laden with the superb produce or when Dad went off to town with a wagonload of fresh fruit and vegetables surplus to our needs, we were proud indeed!

Mother was never a strict adherent to utilitarianism, though. Smack in the middle of our main garden was an overflow of roses, cockscombs, pansies, violets, irises, gladiolus, chrysanthemums, dahlias, and countless other flowers that hadn't found a home in our yard. Mom's devotion to flowers lasted beyond the days when she tended them with care. After her death, Ethel found a copy of the Cole Porter song "Old-Fashioned Garden" in her Bible.

Keeping Our Home Fires Burning

In *Foothold* Dad told the story of how his young family was burned out of house and home when they were living on the George Hiller place in Makanda Township in November of 1913. He did not tell his readers that Mother, her two-year-old toddler, Lester, and one-year-old baby, George, were alone in the house when the flue caught on fire. Or how she evacuated the children first, placing George in a garden row well away from the house for safety and leaving Lester in the yard. Or of the valiant effort she made to save some of the essential household items, bringing out a table first and planting Lester's dress tail under one leg to keep him from following her back inside. Or how Dad arrived from the fields to find smoke billowing skyward from the house and Mom frantic with fear because she couldn't remember, for a moment, what she had done with George!

I'm sure now that Mother told us this story to impress on us the hazards of tending wood-and-coal-burning stoves. We knew it was a serious business, though. Every fall we had a large load of coal delivered for use in our stoves, but we also needed a lot of wood. Every so often, Dad and the boys would take a team down to the woodlot to fell and bring home a few tree trunks to be hand-sawn into bolts about eighteen inches long and then split with an axe into firewood. Watching them set up the final phases of this operation around the chopping block in the backyard was very interesting to me. The felled log was mounted on a sawhorse (a rack with Y-shaped ends) with a sawyer on each end of the two-man saw. After the log was cut into bolts, the axe work began. Swinging the axe with enough precision to split the bolts into varying sizes ranging from kindling wood on up required strength and skill, and doing it without wounding one's self fore and aft seemed a formidable feat, indeed! I greatly admired our woodcutters. So much so that carrying in armloads of their freshly cut and nicely scented wood was a privilege.

There was something about those wood-and-coal-burning stoves that was comforting. But if the fuel was not added evenly and the dampers were not adjusted properly, the stovepipes would overheat. If the pipes were snug, all we had to do was cool things down in a hurry. But, with the heavy traffic in our wood-frame house, the stovepipes sometimes worked themselves apart and needed a tap to pound the joints solidly together.

I have one horrendous memory of such an occasion when Mom literally held a red-hot pipe with her bare hand until George could throw her a nearby towel and pound the pipe into place from its connecting joints above the stove. She was badly burned. We all knew that she had probably saved our house from burning down that evening.

In the summer, our heating stove was disconnected from the flue, polished to a fare-thee-well, and moved to a closet under the staircase. But the kitchen stove continued to see heavy duty three times a day almost every day.

Could She Bake a Cherry Pie?

Feeding her family was a responsibility our mother never took lightly, and no mother ever did it better! Dad reminded me in one of our regular telephone conversations of an occasion that tested more than Mother's culinary skills. One wintry afternoon she had prepared a great pot of backbone and dumplings for our supper. She poured the steaming food into a crock in the center of the kitchen table and set out the rest of the meal. Darkness was coming on swiftly, and she asked Dad to light a lamp. He brought in a lamp from the unheated dining room, touched a match to the wick, and lowered the cold globe slowly into place. But he didn't wait long enough. The globe exploded, showering everything on the table with fragments of glass. Dad told me that Mom never said a word as she cleared the table and went calmly about the business of preparing her second supper that evening. And, thanks to our cellar, which was always full or about to be replenished, it wasn't too much of a chore.

Telling this story literally makes my mouth water, because Mother had a way with dough, be it for dumplings or some other delectable product of her kitchen. Since the first day I tasted her light bread, for instance, all other breads have fallen short. We children knew it was time to make bread when Mother went to the well to bring up her yeast. We loved to watch her knead and pummel the dough and expertly pinch off sections for rising. And when the loaves and rolls were finally ready for the oven, we waited impatiently for that treat of treats.

There were other treats, of course. Like an occasional batch of cinnamon rolls. And raisin, rhubarb, gooseberry, apple, cherry, pumpkin, mince, chocolate, banana cream, and custard pies. And peach, blackberry and, raspberry cobblers. And strawberry shortcake made with pie crusts. These country kitchen bakery goods, turned out on our wood-burning stove, were not our daily fare, though.

As I mentioned, our cellar was a storehouse of canned goods and Irish and sweet potatoes and onions that was replenished each year. Mother began "putting food by" as soon as the garden produce started maturing. She canned sauerkraut, green beans, peas, corn, beets, sweet and dill pickles, green and red peppers, whole tomatoes and juice, red cherries, grape juice, and a variety of berry jams, preserves, and jellies. Many bushels of peaches and apples were brought in from the M&O Fruit Farm to be canned in sections or made into butters. And Mom's canning days, from cut-up to red-hot sealing wax closures, were very interesting. Only once did something dreadful happen. As she twisted a lid tightly onto a glass jar, the jar splintered and a long sliver of glass buried itself in her hand. She had to go to town to have our doctor remove it.

One summer, we tried something very different with a bushel of M&O apples. We placed clean sheets on the metal roof of our chicken house and dried apple sections. As I recall, they looked awful but were quite tasty.

We had other sources of foodstuffs, of course. In the fall, Cleve Hickam brought his molasses mill around to process our cane sugar into thick, sweet sorghum molasses. From our smokehouse came cuts of pork, including ham smoked to perfection by our father. From the chicken house came Mother's chickens. From our pond came fish. From fields came game like rabbits, squirrels, geese, and even opossums. From an occasional bee tree came honey.

Although our daily fare was likely to be beans or potatoes and cornbread or biscuits (with fresh vegetables and fruits in the summer and canned products in the winter), the Sunday fare was bound to be chicken and dumplings and all the trimmings. Or fried chicken. I cannot prepare chicken on a Sunday now without thinking of the dinners Mom prepared for us on the farm. Once, when the feelings were almost overwhelming, I penned a poem to commemorate those special days:

Farm Fest

Sometimes on summer Sundays
I go back to yesterday on the farm . . .
To the old house,
Sparsely furnished
but swept and scrubbed and dusted
from top to bottom . . .
To a slat rocker by the living room window,
lace curtains billowing in the breeze,
and sunlight casting dappled patterns
on the green linoleum floor . . .

To a freshly cut bouquet of roses
lending elegance to an aging library table
and perfuming every corner of the house . . .
And Mom in a flowered, handmade voile,

red-gold tendrils of hair escaping the pins,
her blue eyes alight
and her fine skin flushed in the kitchen heat
as she prepared a feast on a wood-burning stove . . .
The table extended to its full length
and surrounded with a hodgepodge of chairs,
the "good" plates set all around,
and in the center
platters of fried chicken,
great bowls of mashed potatoes and gravy,
fresh green beans,
new peas swimming in cream sauce,
corn on the cob,
sliced tomatoes,
fruit salad,
and banana pudding with meringue topping . . .

A long, lazy afternoon in the front yard,
company dropping by,
unhurried talk,
and frequent trips to a large crock of tea
cooled with chunks of ice
brought all the way from town . . .
I remember how good it felt going down.

But, of course, with a diverse brood of children in various stages of development, preparation of our regular meals was not the end of it. Lunches, many lunches, had to be prepared. I recall how pleasurable it was to contemplate the contents of my dinner bucket during books at school. There might be a fried egg on a biscuit (how clever of McDonald's to copy my 1930s school lunch special);

a hard-boiled egg with a little waxed paper packet of salt and pepper; pork and beans in a small glass jar; a potato cake made from supper leftovers; pickles in waxed paper; fried-apple turnovers; raisin pie; fresh tomatoes, apples, peaches, and grapes; potted ham on a biscuit; peanut butter and jelly on light bread; ham or tenderloin or fried chicken; homemade cookies or cake; and, occasionally, store-bought Fig Newtons or candy. And, sometimes, something totally different. A surprise!

Lunches had to be prepared for Lester and George during the ten years from their early teens to their early twenties that they worked at the M&O, too. In the winters, they took their lunches with them. But in the summers, we younger children took turns carrying hot lunches to them. It was not far; and the twisting, turning, uphill, downhill route to the M&O was always interesting. Once, as I trudged the dusty road, I found a huge snake coiled smack in my path. I gave that snake a very wide berth by crawling under a fence and going several yards before I got back on the road. We found out later that the younger Ellis boys (their family lived on the Modglin farm at the time) were trying to give one of us a scare and were, indeed, hiding in the roadside bushes at the time to witness the reaction. Lucky me!

The plain and simple truth is, our mother was a very fine preparer of foods. Again, Dad summed it up perfectly when he said, "Each and every meal is a culinary delight!"

Shave and a Haircut

Everyone acknowledged that our mother had about the most glorious hair ever seen. When she was younger, it was a glossy auburn that enhanced her peaches-and-cream complexion and sky-blue eyes. As she grew older, it merely changed to the strawberry blond hue that females try in vain to achieve from a bottle. And it was curly, mind you.

Frank Joseph and Edith Pearl Cluster Mileur and their eight children in a Christmas 1933 photograph when the family lived on the M&O Fruit Farm, so called because of its proximity to the Mobile and Ohio Railroad switching station at Etherton Switch. In the first row (*left to right*) are Frank Jewel, Max Grant, Alma Marie, Oma Mae (with baby, Evasue, on her lap), and Ruth. Standing in the back row are Joseph Alexander, Frank, Edith, and Billie Alene. From 1930 to 1947, Frank managed the M&O Fruit Farm, which was typical of southern Illinois fruit farms with its several hundred acres of prime hilltop land devoted mainly to peach and apple crops. The Mileur sons all served in World War II and came back to Murphysboro to buy small fruit farms of their own while holding other jobs and to become active in political and civic affairs. The Mileur daughters all married area men. Edith died in 1946 at fifty-three years of age. Frank, whose ancestors came from France to America in the late 1870s to settle first in the French quarter of East St. Louis and finally in Murphysboro Township, was ninety-two when he died in 1985.

The author's mother, Bessie Mae, as a young lady with her beautiful auburn hair arranged over a "rat." Worn by women of fashion at the turn of the century, the rats were generally made from the combings of one's own hair. The author recalls her mother telling a story of two gypsies who paid a surprise visit to her home on the Matt Modglin farm and went away with one item—the rat made of her own auburn hair. The gypsies were members of the caravan who encamped along the roadway near Etherton Switch to put on their traveling show in the pasture of the Modglin farm for the neighborhood people.

I was the only one in the family who did not inherit a single one of Mother's multiple blessings (Ethel once hinted that I must have been adopted). My hair was glossy enough but coal black and straight as a stick, as they say. For the occasional special event, Mother would heat up the curling iron in the globe of the kerosene lamp and try valiantly to make me some curls. This was a tedious process, as the iron had to be heated and then tested on paper. If the paper smoked, the iron was too hot. If it didn't curl with the heat, the iron wasn't hot enough. This was not a job to be undertaken often, so for the most part my hair remained straight.

When I was about seven or eight years old, women in our community began to get permanent waves in beauty parlors in town. I got the one and only perm that I have ever endured the spring that I graduated from grade school. No astronaut was ever tethered to a more formidable looking contraption. It seemed, especially after you were all connected, like a surefire way to get yourself electrocuted. And I did get a badly burned scalp and a frizz that only time could heal. I learned a valuable lesson in that "beauty" shop. What you can't do with pins and rollers simply should not be done!

When I was tall enough to reach Grandpa's head as he relaxed in an easy chair or in a lawn chair in the front yard, he would pay me a penny an hour for combing his hair. I doubt if I ever worked a full hour. As soon as he fell asleep, I would steal away. I never really minded doing it, though. He seemed to enjoy it so much. And I learned at an early age how to part, smooth, and shape the hair with a comb.

I got some more sophisticated practice one day when Mom had gone to town. Ethel and I decided to curl Betty's hair like Shirley Temple's. Since we didn't have regular curlers, we rolled her hair very tightly on fasteners from A&P 8 O'Clock coffee sacks. It worked. When we finished with her, she looked more like Shirley Temple than Shirley herself, spit curl and all. Ethel and I didn't know at the time that some of Shirley's curls were fakes that had to be stuck on her head. Had we known, I am certain we would have tried that, too.

The next step was learning to do one's own barbering. We were all more or less talented in that department, or became so with practice. Dad cut Grandpa's hair. Mom cut Dad's and the boys' sometimes, but Raymond "Peck" and Albert "Buddy" Greathouse's barbershop (in the log cabin back across the field where they lived) was also available to the menfolk of our family. They could get a professional haircut there for twenty-five cents. And, of course, Mom also cut the hair of the five younger children. Essentially, boys and girls got the same cut, except the boys' ears were more exposed. I must have liked our country version of the flapper bob with bangs and a shingled back, because I have worn a longer, modified form of the original cut ever since.

Once the hair was cut and there were a million tiny slivers down your collar, there was nothing for it but a bath. There is no need to re-create here the often-told tale of the wintertime washtub-behind-the-stove routine. Since privacy was valued above all else in our family, we created some new scenarios. Like braving the frigid clime of the upstairs with a teakettle of scalding-hot water to heat things up as your tub cooled down (it wasn't that bad if you stayed within range of the radiant heat from the flue). And there were a number of warm-weather options. You could dangle your feet in one of the natural basins in the rock-lined creek bed just down the hill back of the house and let the tumbling waters rinse them clean. You could wash away the cares of the day in our very fine spring-fed and well-drained pond. Or, if the notion struck you, you could steal away for a bath or shower in a nearby woodland bower known as Twin Rock, where Sugar Creek meandered through and over rock outcroppings to form a lovely waterfall and a rock-lined pool. And when Wayne came home from service, he converted our deceased grandfather's small room to a bath, with a tub and lavatory and a rudimentary but adequate drainage system. So we were prepared to follow John Wesley's admonition that "cleanliness is, indeed, next to godliness." When we went off to church on Sundays, even our shoelaces had been scrubbed.

The haircutting process was an occasional thing. Shaving was the time-consuming grooming exercise in our house. With a houseful of men who shaved every day, and growing boys eager to get into the act, one could watch the various steps with regularity. Dad was very good with a razor strop, a flat strip of leather used to hone the straight edge of the razor. The metal hook at the top of the strop was attached to a chair round, a liberal helping of spit was applied to the strop, and the razor was moved up and down rhythmically until it was sharp enough to sheer off an arm hair just like that. At one time there were four men using that same razor daily, so the stropping had to be done fairly often. I can still hear the whop, whop, whop of that razor against the hard leather.

Then She Laid Us Down to Sleep

> They say that man is mighty,
> He governs land and sea,
> He wields a mighty scepter
> O'er lesser powers that be:
> But a mightier power and stronger
> Man from his throne has hurled,
> And the hand that rocks the cradle
> Is the hand that rules the world.
>
> —William Ross Wallace (1819–81)

Have you ever lain down in a pile of newly mown hay? Or, better yet, on a mattress plump with a stuffing of that sweet-smelling herbage? In the early years at the home place, we had ornamental cast-iron beds buttressed with wooden slats that didn't always stay put and sometimes clattered to the floor in the middle of the night. Springs, which bore little resemblance to those used today, rested on the slats. And then came the straw mattress and feather pillows. Mother seamed up the heavy cotton ticking fabric for the mattresses and pillows. Feathers, of course, were saved assiduously for the pillows and lasted much longer than the straw. It had to be stirred and replumped or even replaced periodically. Nevertheless, when we lay down on that crunchy, aromatic surface, a pleasant sleep was assured. When store-bought mattresses came into use in our home, I was not at all sure at first if I liked them, but Mother was bent on progress.

One winter, the tried-and-true weather indicators—woolly worms and assorted other animals, and plants as well—foretold the severe weather predicted by the *Farmer's Almanac*. Mother decided we would need extra bedding. This was to be quite a chore, since there were six beds in the house and the goal was a warm coverlet for every bed.

Shortly thereafter, she came back from town with a quilting frame, large rolls of cotton filler, several yards of cotton flannel for backing, and a few balls of yarn. A great box of hand-me-down, outgrown, or simply worn-out woolen garments was brought down from upstairs and thoroughly aired in the out-of-doors. Then we cut and ripped the garments apart with razor blades. Mother sorted out the good pieces, cut out the damaged places, pressed the pieces with a flat iron, and sewed them together on her treadle sewing machine. She made no attempt to cut the available fabric into squares, and the end result was an abstract design that appeared to have been planned.

Then the quilting frame was hung from the crossbeams in the living room next to the stove. The flannel backing, the cotton filler, and the chalk-marked quilt top were secured in the frame, and we proceeded to thread through and tie off rows and rows of pretty "butterflies" with colorful yarn. Then Mother hand-stitched the cover down over the backing, and we were through!

The winter was bitterly cold. And our bedrooms were unheated, of course. But I remember distinctly that when Mother tucked me in under one of our comforters of many colors, I felt, to quote one Benjamin Franklin, as "snug as a bug in a braided rug."

Part Four ❧ Fledglings in Flight

One Little Indian

My *Webster's* defines "rock hound" as an amateur rock and mineral collector. I suppose that I was about as amateurish a collector as could be found, but surely there were none as devoted to the cause as I.

Dad had a few Indian relics, flintstones mostly, that he had unearthed while cultivating the fields of the home place. Once, when we were looking at them, he told us a story his mother had told him when he was about five years old, a very romantic story about an ancestor who had gone on a buffalo hunt in the Oklahoma Territory. While there, he had seen a beautiful Indian maiden in a village where they stopped. Back home in Tennessee, he could not forget her. Finally, he went back to her village, married her, and brought her home. Unfortunately, there were no genealogy enthusiasts in our family at that time, and the story, although widely circulated in various branches of the family then and now, was never authenticated. Authentic or not, the story fell on fertile ground in our home, and Indian relics became my passion.

The fascinating thing was that our farm had obviously been the home place of some earlier Americans, too. Directly across the road there were two Indian mounds. When Dad rented this piece of land and cultivated it, he always plowed around the mounds, saying that they were sacred and should not be disturbed. The county road graders who came through occasionally were not concerned with the fact that they might disturb long-buried artifacts. While their grading wreaked havoc in our honeysuckle-encrusted lane, it did make my archaeological digs very accessible. All I had to do was hang onto the five- or six-foot-high embankments as best I could and pick up the uncovered treasures. I found flintstones of all sizes and shapes and a few beads, too, from which I made myself a little bracelet. I hollowed out the centers of the beads with a needle and then threaded them onto a piece of flexible wire. I wore the bracelet secretively and imagined myself an Indian "princess" like my mysterious ancestor.

One day Dad and the boys brought up a load of rock from a creek bed to pave our driveway. Thereafter, I spent many an hour flat on my stomach on the rocky surface, lost in my new adventure. Gradually, I built up quite a creditable collection. I say that for good reason. A curator from Southern Illinois Normal University's museum came by one summer afternoon. The subject of my Indian relics came up as the lady and my mother talked. My collection was then examined, and some of the pieces were declared to be of museum quality. I, wanting to at least appear magnanimous in such impressive company, gave my best pieces to her. But that evening, as the old saying goes, I cried my heart out. Dad insisted on knowing why. He said nothing then, but years later (sometime early in the 1970s) he gave me his small but important collection of Indian artifacts uncovered in a lifetime of farming at the home place. Eventually, I decided to have an expert examine the relics. Michael J. McNerney, who was then the president of American Resources Group, Ltd., of Carbondale, verified for me that some of the pieces were indeed noteworthy.

Recalling this story and researching the background have given me much food for thought. And, in my mind's eye, I can clearly see a lithe bronze figure with moccasin-clad feet treading softly among the wildflowers and willows of my home place in the long, long ago.

Indian artifacts found by the author's father while tilling fields at the home place and by the author during her early archaeological activities. Cultural affiliations and age of the artifacts are (A) Dalton—ten thousand years old, (B) Early Archaic—eight thousand years old, (C) Late Archaic—four thousand years old, and (D) Woodland-Mississippian—two thousand years old. The area's first human inhabitants were the Paleo-Indians, a far ranging hunting and foraging society that developed stone implements similar to the older artifacts shown here. A later group, the Indians of the Mississippian culture—who lived in this area from 900 A.D. to the 1500s and specialized in agriculture—produced finely made arrow and spear heads, beautiful pottery and statuary, and farming implements such as the hoe pictured in part D.

A Spoonful of Sugar

None of us children ever received vaccinations of any kind and somehow escaped the major diseases. Lester's tonsils were removed when he was about five years of age, and he almost hemorrhaged to death. The rest of us kept our tonsils. And Mother came close to perfecting the family practice specialty long before the medical world caught on. With one exception, she was the only doctor who treated me until I left home at the age of eighteen. The exception was a bad cut that required some stitches.

My first brush with Mother's skills occurred when I was about four years old. I was helping Dad with the cream separating process when we still had the separator in our cellar beneath the house. While he was concentrating on turning the handle of the separator, I found an interesting metal guard that slid to one side to reveal a gear box with all kinds of little wheels whirling around and meshing in a fascinating way. As I was inspecting this marvel, one finger somehow got in the gear box, and I was in big trouble. When my mother saw the multiple lacerations and realized the possible consequences, she took me to town to see Dr. Horstman, our family physician. He recommended the removal (to the first joint) of my mangled finger. My mother declined, gathered me up and took me home to practice her own brand of medicine. There were long hours of hot saltwater baths and around-the-clock applications of a Vaseline-turpentine poultice. Gradually, the finger healed. The nail continued to come off for several years, but the end result was a completely normal finger with barely discernible flesh and nail scars.

One day in 1932, we children came home from school to find that a bed had been set up in the living room. Dad was in it. And badly hurt. The team of horses had been spooked by something, and the wagon they were pulling overturned and trapped Dad beneath it. The team dragged him all the way to the fence and then stopped. He suffered shoulder and ankle injuries and what was diagnosed as "a loose kidney." But Mom nursed him back to health in short order.

There were other notable examples of her healing techniques. Like the time when Wayne developed a severe case of rheumatism. She treated him by immobilizing his limbs with wrapped ears of corn steamed in their husks. Or the time a bullet, fired, no doubt, by an unskilled or careless hunter, grazed deeply across Lester's forehead as he stood in our front yard. Or the time the head of a protruding spike nail penetrated my thigh as I fell from a beam in the empty hayloft in the barn. Or the time we children came back from a foray into the neighbor's pasture with Ethel mortally wounded, we thought. While investigating some bushes, something bit her on the thumb. Charley, sure, as we all were, that the perpetrator was a deadly snake, slit her finger with his pocket knife to make it bleed. Mom had the double problem of treating a possible snakebite and preventing blood poisoning from the rusty knife. She judged, correctly, that Ethel had a bad sting instead of a snakebite, but her treatment did include the application of some medicinal alcohol. After a while, Ethel healed up nicely.

Eventually, Mom's exploits in the field of medicine became known to the community so that people brought their problems to her. Like the day Mrs. Grammer brought little Joe Dean over after he had swallowed a penny. I was very interested in this diagnosis. And, sure enough, Mrs. Grammer came back in a day or so to tell Mom that the penny had, indeed, appeared as promised. Mom, who had assisted Mrs. Grammer in Joe Dean's delivery, had a special stake in seeing that he prospered.

Only once do I remember a sort of shockwave of worry in our home about our health. We learned that Vivian Morefield, who lived with her family on the old Lon Hagler place next door, had become partially paralyzed. The doctor finally diagnosed the paralysis as a complication of the bone felon Vivian had in her finger. Sometime later, when a fully recovered Vivian came over to play, we knew that all was well.

The only potentially dangerous disease we had as children was the measles. All five of us younger children had them one winter. A double bed was set up next to the stove in the living room, and we all slept crosswise in it. Mom did the day care, and Dad kept the night watch. I remember lying very still, while feeling utterly miserable and fussy enough to raise the roof, because I didn't want to disturb Dad as he tried to nap a little in the rocker by the fire.

We did, of course, have the usual colds caught from classmates at school. When we all came down with a sore throat, Mom would come around at night with a spoonful of sugar laced with several drops of medicinal turpentine for each of us. It worked. Usually, if our condition worsened, we were moved to a cot by the living room stove for chest rubs of Vicks salve. Or a bad-smelling product called Ozone that Mother got from the Raleigh man, followed by the application of heated flannel cloths. After a day or so of the Ozone treatment, one was willing to feign improvement or even recovery.

Actually, we were very healthy. Of course, we had the usual gamut of childhood ailments. Tummy aches were eased with hot ginger tea. Sluggish digestive tracts were helped along with syrup of pepsin. Infected eyes were bathed in hot salt water. Sweet oil was heated in a spoon on the stove and funneled into aching ears. The cathartic properties of castor oil and Epsom salts were utilized frequently. The salts were also used in hot baths for sprained ankles. And axle grease made a marvelously soothing salve for skinned and scraped knees and elbows. Whatever our ailments, we just knew that Mom could fix it.

A 1946 photograph of William and Elzora Warfield Morefield, who lived on the Lon Hagler place, just north of the author's home place, from 1929 to 1932. William was born March 1, 1882, in Ashland, Kentucky, to Thomas and Mary Moore Morefield. Elzora was born June 5, 1887, in rural Butler County, Missouri, to William and Martha Dare Warfield. William and Elzora were married in Poplar Bluff, Missouri, in 1904 and moved in 1906 to southern Illinois, where their children—Ellie, Esther, Vivian, Opal, Jesse, Vernon, Charles, John, Colleen, and Eunice—were born. Three other children—two girls born in Missouri and Vernon's twin brother—died in infancy. William, of Irish descent and a farmer all his life, died in March 1960 at seventy-eight years of age; Elzora, of Native American ancestry and a skilled baker and seamstress, was seventy-six when she died in February 1964. Sean William Morefield and Ann Caraway Morefield, the author's grandnephew and grandniece, are the great grandchildren of William and Elzora.

Sometimes, one of Mother's assistants had to fill in for her. I have an image now of twenty-year-old George gently removing grains of corn from two-year-old Betty's nose when she wouldn't let anyone else near her. Unnoticed, she had stuffed her nose full of the grains. Then, when she found she couldn't breathe, she became hysterical.

Our mother was no slouch as a dentist, either. She used camphorated oil to relieve teething pain. The daily brushings with salt and baking soda that she encouraged must have been the ticket to dental health because most of us were never in a dentist's office until we were in our early twenties. The few toothaches that did occur were treated with cotton soaked in camphorated oil and held firmly between the teeth until the pain lessened. And just think of all those baby teeth that she extracted over the years!

Mother continued to develop her impressive program of medical care long after we were grown and no longer living at home. Even now, when I am not well, I can almost feel her cool hand on my fevered brow.

Scrub-a-Dub-Dub

So many of the things that our mother did were things that only she could do. But we could all help with the laundry. And our game plan for the summer operation was almost fun.

Now, this was a many-faceted project. The bench on which the washtubs stood was set up under the smokehouse porch. A solid wall of honeysuckle from the ground up to the edge of the roof overhang made a cooling breezeway for all us willing workers. If our rain barrels were not sufficiently full, water had to be carried up from the well at the bottom of our hill. An open fire had to be built under boilers to ensure a ready supply of hot, sudsy water (Fels-Naptha soap was shaved into the water for the necessary suds) for boiling of sheets, pillow cases, white shirts, underwear, socks, et cetera. Every now and then, Mother would utilize ingredients generated in our household (lard and ashes plus lye) to make a very fine soap for use on items requiring a heavy-duty cleanser. And starch had to be cooked on the cookstove in the house and brought out to be strained into a container of water (bluing was added to whiten the whites and brighten the brights). Clothes progressed from a washboard scrubbing to a cool rinsing, to starching (if they were to be ironed).

The clean clothes were hung out on lines and, occasionally, along sections of fencing if we ran out of line space. The sweet-smelling clothes were taken in and folded, or sprinkled down and rolled up in a basket for ironing. Ironing with flat irons heated on the kitchen stove required some expertise, but, with practice, the skill came.

To get to the crux of this story, I must digress a bit. Our parents were of the opinion that children should not be burdened with the unwholesome conduct of some adult members of our population. If you cared to listen, however, you could hear some very interesting conversations between our parents and older siblings about wrongdoers all the way from John Dillinger, America's "Public Enemy No.1," to the rival Birger and Shelton gangs operating in our neighboring Williamson County to moonshiners and revenuers operating in our own Jackson County. Of more immediate interest to all of us, though, were the rumors that strangers had been popping up here and there in the community with no legitimate excuses for being there.

Sure enough, one summer day our country-style laundromat was rudely invaded. There, in our very own driveway, was a car we'd never seen before. Three men eased themselves out of the car and stood there looking things over. Mother peered through the honeysuckle vines for a minute or so, picked up the butcher knife she used to shave the soap, told us children to stay where we were, and motioned for Ol' Fritz to follow her. She advanced up the drive with the butcher knife held behind her back as Ol' Fritz growled menacingly by her side. The three men climbed hastily back into the car and backed out of our drive in a hurry. Mother acted as if it was all a mistake on their part, as if maybe they were lost or something.

Many years later, I was surprised to learn that Mother had never mentioned this incident to Dad. She had simply handled the intruders with the same determination she had displayed when a would-be pantry raider appeared at her Pisque Hollow cabin in Makanda Township (a story related by Dad in *Foothold*), and that was the end of it.

One summer, late in the 1930s, we launderers got an unexpected windfall. Mother had seen a nifty wooden washing machine in town. A handle controlled the agitator, and all you had to do was stand there and move the handle back and forth. Grandpa, knowing that we really needed the washer and that Mom couldn't afford it, bought it for her with his Old-Age Assistance money. After that, washdays were a snap, summer *and* winter.

Mother Get Your Gun

The marksmen in our family had some competition. Our mother was a markswoman. Lester and George had to hustle to outshoot her in tin-can target practice sessions. I can't remember a time when our rifle and shotgun were kept anywhere but in the corner of the kitchen next to the backdoor. Any wild game venturing into our yard or air space were really asking for it and often ended up on our table as a result of their carelessness.

A fine display of Mom's shooting skills came one bright spring day. We suddenly heard the harsh, repetitive cries of the blue jay who was nesting in the big elm in the front yard. We all ran out to investigate the cause of her frantic chatter. Mom finally saw a huge blacksnake lying along the limb near the jay's nest. She ran back and got the rifle, took aim, and fired. Down came a cleanly severed branch and one very dead snake. She didn't get there in time to save the baby jays, but she may have saved others.

Once a great white crane got as far as the pond on our farm and then died of a gunshot wound someone had inflicted upon it. I remember being stunned with this wanton killing. And I began to form an unfavorable impression of those who would kill animals for sport alone.

I remember only too well the one time I decided I'd like to know how to handle a gun. Under my mother's tutelage, I fitted the shotgun firmly against my shoulder, sighted down the barrel, and pulled the trigger. The roar of the blast was deafening, and I was thrown to the ground in an ignominious heap. With that experience to guide me, my gun-shy days began!

Those Magnificent Flying Machines

> Up, up the long delirious burning blue
> I've topped the wind-swept heights with easy grace,
> Where never lark, or even eagle, flew;
> And, while with silent, lifting mind I've trod
> The high untrespassed sanctity of space,
> Put out my hand, and touched the face of God.
>
> —John Gillespie Magee Jr., *High Flight*

Our early fascination with the heavens extended to the occasional airships that flew in them. And, of course, news of aircraft and their daring pilots got our attention. When Captain Charles A. Lindbergh became the hero of the hour after his solo, nonstop, thirty-three-and-one-half hour flight across the Atlantic from New York to Paris in the *Spirit of St. Louis* in May 1927, I was only two years old. But his was not a deed that faded quickly into the background. In the next few years, I overheard and absorbed many a conversation around our supper table or in after-supper discussions on the subject. So that, when the two-year-old son of Charles and Anne Morrow Lindbergh was kidnapped in 1932, I was well aware of the shock and concern of my family for the great aviator and his wife. We kept abreast of the dramatic and notorious "crime of the century" by listening to the evening news on our radio and by reading our newspaper. Bruno Richard Hauptmann figured prominently in our lives for a long, long while.

That same year, Amelia Earhart, "America's darling," flew her own solo transatlantic flight. I was seven years old and had a heroine of my very own. I followed the news avidly for word of her exploits as she continued to set records regularly. And I was not alone. When Amelia and her navigator went down in the Pacific in 1937, she was probably the most popular woman in the world. This dramatic event happened when I was twelve years old, and I will never forget the shock of the news.

That same year (May 6, 1937) the nation and the world were shocked by the news that the German dirigible *Hindenburg* had crashed on arrival at Lakehurst Naval Air Station in southern New Jersey. The 804-foot-long airship exploded in a ball of fire as it began to moor, killing thirty-five of its passengers and crewmen and one Navy man on the ground. The firsthand account on Chicago radio station WLS of the disaster was broadcast repeatedly across the nation. This was a particularly poignant event for us because a great zeppelin had floated majestically over our farm one day while we went crazy below, waving and yelling ourselves hoarse until it was well out of sight. So we had actually seen a ship like *The Hindenberg*. The disaster was real!

And none of us had forgotten another aviation disaster that occurred two years earlier. Wiley Post had completed the first around-the-world flight in 1933. So we were well aware of his fame and that of his good friend, Will Rogers, easily the most popular man in America. We were playing in the yard the fateful day (August 15, 1935) when we got the word that Post and Rogers, en route to Siberia, had gone down and were killed in a crash near Point Barrow, Alaska. We were terribly saddened at this news. We knew well there would not likely be another Will Rogers. And Wiley Post, a Native American from Oklahoma, was a daring man, indeed.

But these disasters only made us more aware of those magnificent flying machines. Any plane in our air space got our undivided attention. One day Ethel came running in to tell us that a plane was "putting out white stuff." We all rushed out only to find that some enterprising soul was doing a little aerial advertising to enlighten us country folk. Not that we were disappointed, exactly, but the thought of a crash in our pasture did hold out some intriguing possibilities.

With all this activity in our air space and elsewhere, it was perfectly natural that we would get some ideas of our own about flying. Betty, perhaps our most adventurous sibling, decided that she could do it without benefit of man-made appendages. So one fine day she climbed onto the roof of the chicken house and jumped off. In her in-flight trajectory, her out-flung hand hit the sharp edge of the corrugated metal roof. She made it back to the house, but Mom had another medical emergency to handle. She cleansed the wound, treated it with medicinal turpentine, and bandaged it securely. The next morning Betty walked into the kitchen and promptly fainted. But after a few days home from school, the zigzag cut healed, the numb fingers came back to life, and all was well.

Charley had an eye to the sky, too, and engineered an attempted takeoff from the loft of a neighbor's barn with the help of homemade wings. Miraculously, no one was seriously hurt.

But the pièce de résistance was the airplane Wayne built, which had an almost successful test flight. Wayne used two metal barrels and the motor from an abandoned car. The plane had a propeller, a rudder, wings, wheels, tail flaps, a cockpit up front, and a passenger seat. As Charley and Wayne taxied down an incline in the pasture one day in their airplane and finally came to a halt, Wayne said, "Did you feel that? We almost had a liftoff!" Mom put a stop to this project when she realized the potential for a disaster of our own.

Our interest in flying did not diminish as a result of these escapades. Even Mom seemed to catch the vision when a man who owned a Piper Cub brought the plane to Murphysboro. He ferried passengers on short pleasure flights over the immediate countryside for a nominal fee (a penny per pound) from a rough landing strip east of Riverside Park. One Saturday, our brothers took Mom there to have a look. She paid her fee without hesitation, donned her goggles, and climbed in to become the first real flying member of the Caraway clan. It gives me great joy to dwell on this adventurous side of our mother's character and to report that she took a second flight into the wild blue yonder that very day.

And so, with the possible exception of Douglas "Wrong Way" Corrigan, who said he was going to fly from New York to California in 1938 but landed at Baldonnel, Ireland, twenty-eight hours later, our family was quite taken with flyers of the day and airships in general.

A Battle Hymn of the Republic

As a child studying the momentous events of the Civil War in our one-room school, I had fixed my mind on the absolute necessity of preserving the Union and on President Lincoln's agony, eloquence, and eventual martyrdom in the cause. But the Confederate general of generals, Robert E. Lee, marched across the pages of my history book with such grace and valor that he, too, was enshrined forever in my heart.

There were Civil War figures closer to home for me, though. Grandpa Caraway often told us after-supper stories of how his parents, William and Mary Jane Caraway, brought their five children (including Grandpa) up from Wilson County, Tennessee, to Saline County in southern Illinois at the onset of the war. Grandpa was only a small child at the time of the exodus, but he remembered it well. And this story was retold, as Grandpa's brothers and sisters had recollected it and passed it on to their descendants, when our Caraway cousins from Saline County and various other points in southern Illinois came to call. Since I never saw any of my six great-aunts and -uncles (two more children were born to William and Mary Jane in Illinois), I relished the stories my grandfather, father, and cousins told of these colorful and long-lived southern Illinois pioneers.

From time to time down through the years, I found myself thinking about those family members who had not come northward during the conflict. Finally, I began making inquiries concerning the Caraways from Tennessee who had fought for the Confederacy. Thelma Caraway Landrum, of Columbus, Georgia, the author of *Some Carraway-Caraway Families*, sent me some information taken from *Tennesseeans in the Civil War: A Military History of the Confederate Union*, published by the University of Tennessee Press. Eleven Caraway, six Carraway, and six Carroway names appeared on the Confederate rosters in the reference. Nine Caraway, Carraway, and Cariway men from Tennessee were also listed on the Federal rosters. This proof of our own family's agony in that period only reinforced my appreciation of all kindred tales.

A copy of a tintype taken of Mary Jane Clemmons and William P. Caraway on the occasion of their wedding in Wilson County, Tennessee, December 18, 1846. William and Mary Jane were the author's paternal great-grandparents. As Union sympathizers, the family came north from Tennessee to settle near Eldorado in Saline County, Illinois, in the early months of the Civil War.

Church in the Wildwood

The Holy Bible was the most cherished piece of literature in our home. And our names were all inscribed in it on a special page. Along with little Bible stories, we learned at our mother's knee of her high regard for Makanda's Reverend Henry Ward Beecher (the Methodist minister) and the Reverend E. H. Zipprodt (the Baptist minister who officiated at her wedding).

My own earliest memory of a church experience was memorizing the Lord's Prayer for recitation in

William Franklin and Nellie Mae Gates Caraway and daughter, Madge, in a photograph taken in 1899 in Eldorado, Illinois. "Willie" was a grandson of William P. and Mary Jane Caraway and a first cousin of the author's father.

our Sunday school class held in the cool basement of Mount Pleasant Methodist Church. I studied those lines with great determination. I mean, it would have been so embarrassing to be unable to recite the Lord's Prayer in His very own house. I remember feeling almost giddy with relief, though, when I was skipped over and did not have to prove myself that morning. No matter—the words had made a permanent groove in my brain, and they are still there.

Lester and George attended the Crab Orchard Christian Church southwest of Carbondale and within walking distance of our home place in their early years. A fork in our country lane to what is now West Pleasant Hill Road took them directly to the church. When they were eighteen and seventeen years of age, they began attending Mount Pleasant because all their friends went there. As we younger children grew big enough to take care of ourselves, we went along with them. Mount Pleasant was some distance from our home, and we traveled north on Route 127 and east and north on what is now Chautauqua and Country Club Roads to get there. Driving the tree-lined country lanes on a sunny Sunday morning was an experience in itself. And this picturesque little church was peopled with other large families like our own. During the 1930s, the congregation included members of the Allen, Applegate, Blessing, Byars, Caraway, Crowell, Davis, Deason, Etherton, Golliher, Heininger, Higgs, Hinchcliff, Hubbs, Huppert,

Jenkins, Jones, Lirely, Murray, Nausley, Neal, Robinson, Trobaugh, Waller, and Whittenberg families.

Sometime after Lester and George married and left home (1935 and 1936), we five younger children began going to the Crab Orchard Church, which was nearer our home. There were memorable families there, too, and Ethel, Charley, and I became members in 1939. At that time, members of the Brewer, Crawshaw, Crowell, Grammer, Haney, Lingle, Lipe, Thomas, and Waller families were the chief supporters of the church, and the Reverend William H. Lirely was pastor.

Crab Orchard, like Mount Pleasant, was a place where people sang. Songs like

> O come to the church in the wildwood,
> O come to the church in the vale,
> No spot is so dear to my childhood
> As the little brown church in the vale.

The Vienna Choir Boys have been singing since six years after Columbus discovered America. And remember the Robert Shaw Chorale? Still, to me, those choirs combined could not possibly make a sound as sweet as was the blend of young and old voices as we sang the great hymns like "Amazing Grace," "Rock of Ages," "The Old Rugged Cross," "Shall We Gather at the River?," "What a Friend We Have in Jesus," and "The Ninety and Nine."

Once a year Crab Orchard really came into its own. The church's Memorial Day dinner-on-the-grounds and afternoon songfest was an event that drew everybody in our immediate area and many from surrounding communities as well.

There was nothing like it anywhere! After the morning service, the little girls, dressed in organdy dresses with matching hair ribbons, marched solemnly to the nearby cemetery with flowers for the graves. Then the basket dinners were spread on a long table under a grove of trees, and everybody partook. When

The Mount Pleasant Methodist Episcopal Church South, established on a one-acre plot in the Casper R. Trobaugh farm west of Carbondale early in the 1870s as an offshoot of the Pleasant Grove Methodist Church on then Route 13 between Carbondale and Murphysboro. Political tensions at Pleasant Grove drove the Democrats in the congregation to split from the "Republican Church" and form the new branch, Mount Pleasant. The first building, aptly nicknamed "Board shanty," was built about 1872 and included a six-by-eight-foot rostrum, a bench made of rough lumber in front of the rostrum where penitents could pray, a similar bench against the wall for the preacher to sit on, kerosene lamps fastened to the wall, and a large wood-burning stove. A new building, properly weatherboarded and sealed, was erected on the site in 1904. This second building, heated with a coal-burning stove and lit with acetylene lamps, was destroyed by fire in 1926. The third building, shown here, was erected on the same site in 1927. A gas furnace and other modern conveniences were added over the years to the church for the comfort of the congregation, and the old pews were carefully restored as part of a conscious effort to maintain the charm and originality of the 1927 building. The Mount Pleasant Church was closed July 26, 1998.

The Deasons at their home place in 1932. They were one of the mainstay families of the community around the Mount Pleasant Methodist Church, where Mr. Deason taught Sunday School for many years. *From left to right, first row*, are Herbert Ezbon, Frances Elva, Francis Ellery, Dorothy Lee, Elva Ann, and Raymond Ellery. *Second row*: Glenn Elwood, Lester Allen, Mary Aileen, Ernest Wilburn, and Russell Francis. Another daughter, Alice, died in infancy. Francis Ellery Deason, whose ancestors came from Lithuania in the mid-1800s and migrated to southern Illinois from Tennessee, was born October 13, 1877, in this farming community in Murphysboro Township. Ellery married Elva Ann Winchester of Thomasboro, Illinois, in 1906, and they moved to the Philippines, where he had accepted a position. In 1910 he returned to the States with his family and bought an eighty-acre farm near his birthplace, where they would live the rest of their lives. Elva died in 1949 at sixty-four years of age, and Ellery died at eighty in 1958. Their eldest daughter, Mary, married the author's eldest brother, Lester, in 1935.

we could make it back up the incline to the church, the musical competition began. For that is what it was. There were solos. And duets. And quartets. And they were all accompanied by pianists and guitarists. This went on for hours. Then the community straggled back home to talk about the event until the next year, when it was repeated.

Occasionally we visited Union Hill and Drury, our sister churches in the Southern Illinois Christian Conference, when they hosted conferences or reunions, but Crab Orchard became our home away from home. We had swimming parties and ice cream socials in the summertime and sleigh-riding parties in the wintertime. One sleigh-riding party turned into a nightmare for our parents. Wayne dropped Ethel, Charley, and me off at Bob and Rita Grammer's for the party to be held on the big hill at the back of their farm. The perfect sledding conditions soon deteriorated as a full-fledged snowstorm descended upon us. We barely made it back to the Grammer house, and within minutes the roads were impassible by car or on foot. The entire group of partiers had to bed down on the floor around the heating stove in the living room, and we didn't make it home until midmorning the following day. The Grammers had a telephone then, but we did not. So, even though our parents knew we were in the company of some very responsible people, their only option was to wait and wonder if we were all safe. Dad told me much later that Mom had lain all night on her sleepless bed with one foot on the floor. I think that stormy night precipitated an early maturation in me, and thereafter I went to great lengths to protect Mother from worry.

As I look back now, I remember with great nostalgia how our compact little group kept growing older and drifting away from one another. But I will never forget the pleasantries of our days in our churches in the wildwood. And I have never quite been able to feel at home in any other church. There is something about a place of worship where windows can be flung open and birdsong from a nearby woodland can mingle with the song of the worshipers.

The Crab Orchard Christian Church as it looked when the author and her brothers and sisters attended there in the late 1930s and early 1940s. The original church, called "Little Crab Orchard," was organized on May 31, 1832, at Hiller Cemetery southwest of Carbondale by W. G. Lindsey, R. G. Lindsey, and Simon Hiller, ordained ministers of the Southern Illinois Christian Conference. The log cabin structure that was erected was north of the present church and cemetery. In 1898 Thomas Crawshaw organized the construction of a new church, and he and members of the community erected the building. The church was remodeled in the late 1950s. It closed recently.

A 1966 reenactment of an 1866 scene at Hiller Cemetery, immediately west of the Crab Orchard Christian Church, that inspired the nation's first Memorial Day observance. Taking part in the reenactment are (*from left*) David Lingle, Charlotte Jones, and Donald Gene Caraway (the author's nephew). The idea of honoring the deceased men who had served their country in war was originated at Crab Orchard on Sunday, April 13, 1866, before services, when Civil War veterans Ambrose Crowell, Russell Winchester, and Jonathan F. Wiseman watched a comrade's widow and his children clean his unmarked grave and decorate it with wildflowers. These veterans and members of the congregation decided among themselves that other fallen comrades should also be honored in this way. At a town meeting, the last Sunday in April was chosen as Decoration Day, with Colonel E. J. Ingersoll, a prominent Carbondale businessman and civic leader, as marshal of the day and General John A. Logan as the speaker. The observance at Woodlawn Cemetery on April 29, 1866, was the largest gathering in the history of Carbondale. Two years later, General Logan, commander-in-chief of the Grand Army of the Republic, issued his General Orders No. 11, setting May 30, 1868, as a Memorial Day to be "kept from year to year." The Library of Congress credited General Logan with the creation of Memorial Day, but the Crab Orchard Christian Church laid claim to the nation's first "Decoration Day" by virtue of the fact that the founders first practiced the observance at Hiller Cemetery on April 13, 1866. The church continued the tradition with its own annual Memorial Day observance at Hiller Cemetery, where veterans from the Civil War (three Union and one Confederate) to the Vietnam War are interred. The last such observance was held May 26, 2002.

Part Five ❧ Happy Landings

It Was a Long, Long Way to Carbondale

In May of 1938 I graduated from grade school. That summer our parents hired a carpenter to remodel our house. Earlier, we had obligated ourselves to entertain the Crab Orchard Church Youth Group at our home. We children determined among ourselves not to breathe a word of our renovation to our church friends. We thought it hilarious when our guests began to arrive at our place, only to think they were lost. A neat white one-and-one-half-story cottage stood where the two-and-one-half-story house with its weathered, rough-hewn exterior once stood. That was the last great conspiracy of the five younger Caraways.

In the fall of 1938 I entered University School on the campus of that distant bastion of learning, Southern Illinois Normal University. I rode to school with Roy Reeves, whose family lived on the Modglin farm at the time, often hiking the early dawns and dusks with a lantern to light my way when rain or snow had made our country lane impassible to the inexperienced driver. I do not recall thinking that this was any great trial. Going to high school then was a privilege not available to everyone, and it behooved me to make the most of so excellent an opportunity. Usually, our back roads served us well, as we connected with what is now West Pleasant Hill Road and then drove north on Route 51 to the campus. My schooling would be interrupted, though, when I lost my ride. But again, I was fortunate. Joe and Ruth Mileur, who lived at the M&O Fruit Farm at the time, went to Murphysboro Township High School. I transferred my credits and rode with them for a while, then with another neighbor, and finally had to take a small apartment in town (I paid my rent by working at the Ben Franklin Store on Saturdays and holidays). I completed my high school education there in June of 1943.

A 1939 aerial photograph of Southern Illinois Normal University as it looked when the author entered University School there in the fall of 1938. The laboratory school, which accommodated students through the twelfth grade (the author entered as a high school freshman), was one of the University's early and successful efforts to upgrade educational opportunities in a severely deprived area. Davies Gymnasium, Anthony Hall, the Allyn Building, Shryock Auditorium, Altgeld Hall, and Wheeler Hall, shown clockwise from the top in this photograph, now form the Old Campus of Southern Illinois University Carbondale. Old Main, in the center of the photograph, was destroyed by a fire in 1969.

Murphysboro Township High School, from which the author graduated in June 1943. In the early days of Murphysboro, the children were often instructed by itinerant teachers hired by their parents. The first public school opened in a building on Walnut Street in the mid-1800s, and the Murphysboro High School, with a two-year course of study, was created by the school board of 1883. Sessions were held first in the City Hall and then in other temporary locations (the Bierer Building and the West Side School) until the first Murphysboro Township High School opened for instruction in 1901. The High School, like every other school in Murphysboro except Douglass, was damaged by the 1925 tornado, but repairs were begun immediately. This beautiful building of buff brick with limestone trimming at Twenty-first and Spruce Streets became the home of the Murphysboro Junior High School in 1977, when a new senior high school was constructed on Sixteenth Street and Blackwood Drive. The imposing statue of General John A. Logan that was erected in 1930 still guards its entrance.

The 1942–43 Senior Council at Murphysboro Township High School (*front row, left to right*: Elizabeth Evans, Geraldine Parmley, and the author; *back row*, Allan Lollar, Robert Babb, and Harry Ray). The council was the first form of student government in the history of the school, and members were elected by the senior class. The author is wearing one of her own creations. She bought the red corduroy fabric and a pattern at Penney's and made the suit on her mother's treadle sewing machine.

A close-up of the author as a seventeen-year-old senior at Murphysboro Township High School. The photograph was taken for the 1942–43 yearbook Crimson and Corn, the brainchild of the Senior Council.

Mae Allen and her beautiful little girl at their farm north of Crab Orchard Christian Church in the spring of 1939 when she was teaching in Sharon School. Mae, born in 1904 in Carbondale Township to Lewis and Hannah Etherton Waller, married Edward Lewis Allen in 1925 and was the mother of three children: Edward Lewis, Bette Louise, shown here, and Robert Paul. A graduate of Southern Illinois Normal University, she taught in Jackson County rural schools from 1931 to 1946 and at other schools in Illinois and in Missouri until her retirement in 1978. Mae died January 2, 1997, in Williamsburg, Virginia, at ninety-two years of age, and is resting at the Mount Pleasant United Methodist Church cemetery with her husband and firstborn son.

So, my childhood days, my wildwood days, were over. I cannot move away from this segment, though, without acknowledging the excellent tutelage of Mae Allen, the last of my elementary teachers. In this petite lady's presence, it seemed entirely possible that her intellect and vitality were contagious. I, as one of the older of her charges, was aware at times that she was deliberately stretching our minds beyond the requirements of our prescribed course of study. And rising to the challenge was something we all wanted to do and even found exciting. She, of course, knew that some of us might not have the chance to further our education in the school systems, and, knowing this, she strove diligently to get us in a learning mode that would last a lifetime, regardless of our circumstances. And, besides, she was fun! Mae was also very resourceful. She once taught reading, writing, and arithmetic from donated Sears, Roebuck, and Company catalogs when her school district was too poor to buy books for the children. She, as did her cousin, Lena Doody, before her, impressed the author with her sterling character and unique ability to add a certain spark to the business of learning. How fortunate we were to have this perceptive lady as our teacher.

We'll Have This to Remember

In *Foothold*, Dad told of our dire circumstances in the 1930s. We children were bound to notice some things. Like the time Dad had to borrow money from Mr. Etherton to buy us shoes for school (he soon paid it back with interest). Or the wax crayons that did not blend as well as the more expensive ones (a small piece of cloth rubbed lightly over the coloring remedied that problem to our satisfaction). So our idyllic existence never actually seemed threatened.

One particular day, though, I found myself alone in the house with my parents. I overheard a kitchen discussion of the terrible drought and how poor our crop prospects were without immediate rain. I was standing in a corner of the bedroom near a towering cabinet where family "treasures" were stored and, with all the earnestness that a four-year-old could muster, I begged God to please send us rain. How strange that I recall the request but not the outcome. I have a calm assurance, though, that the rains came. The gates of heaven could not have prevailed against such a plea! That would have been 1929, the year of the market crash. And it is the only recollection I have of impending disaster.

It is a great and lasting tribute to our parents that they got us through the Great Depression without our ever having realized that we were in one. In fact, I remember telling Mother several times of the plight of some of my schoolmates not as fortunate as we. And she was never too burdened or involved with her own problems to do her level best to help if she could. Somehow, through the years, Mom managed to involve us in extracurricular activities that she thought important. Ethel belonged to a 4-H club one year (I went with her although I was too young to belong to her club). Wayne participated in the Golden Gloves boxing tourneys at the St. Andrew's Catholic Church in Murphysboro for a while. And when *Gone with the Wind* came to the Hippodrome in Murphysboro in 1939, Mom took us all to see it. I had read the riveting book in the dim light of a coal oil lamp in my unheated bedroom, but I was still unprepared for the splendor of this, my very first movie. How our mother survived this event, I'll never know, because for weeks afterward the answer to any sibling-to-sibling question was bound to be, "Frankly, my dear, I don't give a damn."

Another stunning realization comes to me now. Our mother used her vast native intellect to keep us children in an exciting learning pattern even when our teachers were less than inspiring. I remember an occasion when I posed a homework problem to her, one that I had pondered long and hard to no avail. She, seemingly without even thinking about it, gave me a perceptive answer that resolved my quandary. It was as if she had burst an elusive bubble with a pinprick of information she had acquired sometime in her life, and I silently acknowledged that my mother was quite possibly the smartest woman alive. And I will always be grateful to her that she was able to impart her own insatiable hunger for knowledge to the rest of us.

I cannot help but remember, also, those years when Lester and George, only a decade or so older than we, guided us younger children with sure and gentle hands down the road of life. They, themselves, began working, when they were twelve and thirteen years old, at the M&O Fruit Farm with timetables for owning their own land while managing some of southern Illinois' most productive fruit farms for others. But they never failed to make time for the rest of us children, setting superior examples always that invited emulation.

No, we were not an angelic host encamped on a southern Illinois hilltop. There were, of course, the usual sibling rivalries and even an occasional parental tiff. But they barely made superficial dents in our common armor, and we all waxed stronger in the bonds of familial love and struggle as the years went by at our Shangri-la.

A gathering of the clan at the home place during World War II on the occasion of a furlough for Wayne before he went overseas. *Left to right*: Mary (Charley's wife), Jean (George's wife), the author, Mary (Lester's wife), Ethel, Betty, Lester, Charley, Wayne, and Charless. The little girl in front is Norma Ann, Lester's daughter. Betty's "stone-washed" jean overalls were contraband from her brother Charley's wardrobe. Charley and George were about to be drafted.

The author and her sister Betty on a visit to the home place in the early 1940s.

Afterword

Several notable events had crowded themselves into our brief lifetime in rapid succession in the 1930s and 1940s. In 1933, in the midst of the Great Depression, we were fortunate that Franklin Delano Roosevelt was inaugurated as our president. Unfortunately, Adolf Hitler became chancellor of Germany that same year. Ominous reports rumbled out of Europe across our airwaves daily. Soon, the tyrants of the world banded together to begin their conquests of weaker nations. Then, in 1939, American scientists split the atom to release an awesome power hitherto unknown to man. And, on December 7, 1941, the Japanese bombed Pearl Harbor in a dastardly attack that would bring isolationist America once again into a world conflagration.

Our days together dwindled as our nation was enveloped in world-shattering events. All too soon, three members of our family were scattered far and wide. George sailed on a troop ship across the Atlantic to serve with the 1265th Combat Engineer Battalion in England, France, and Germany. Wayne sailed west across the great Pacific to distinguish himself with the 101st Airborne Division in Australia, Okinawa, and then Japan. Young Charley flew northward with the 1385th Air Transport Command to the frozen climes of Labrador, Canada, and then Greenland.

Ethel, then I, and then Betty moved to Carbondale. Dad took a job in the Illinois Ordnance Plant, a huge industrial-military complex developed at the Crab Orchard National Wildlife Refuge in Carterville, Illinois, as part of our nation's war preparation. Lester, who had purchased a farm adjoining the home place, farmed all the Caraway land. And Mother kept the home fires burning for the day when we could all come home again.

Our parents are gone now (Mom died in 1963 and Dad in 1977). As I mentioned in the introduction, their story was told in Dad's classic tale, *Foothold on a Hillside*. Mom's blue eyes would have sparkled. And Dad would have gotten a big kick out of the fact that excerpts, abstracts, and reviews were published in numerous newspapers, journals, and magazines (including the *Journal of American History*, the *Journal of American Folklore*, the *American Anthropologist*, the *American Quarterly*, and the *Library Journal* among others), and that he was listed in volume 125 of *Contemporary Authors*. And think how they would have felt about this message from Sir Robert Fellowes, personal secretary to Queen Elizabeth:

> 7 January 1987
> I am commanded by the Queen to thank you for your letter of 17th December. Her Majesty is delighted to accept a copy of *Foothold on a Hillside* and was deeply touched that your father wished her to receive a copy of his book.

During our nation's Bicentennial Celebration, Queen Elizabeth, in a speech at Williamsburg, Virginia, referred to the Revolutionary War as "that bit of unpleasantness." Dad was totally charmed and told me that she was one "one of the few real women left in the world." He asked me to see that she received a copy of *Foothold*. The Southern Illinois University Press conveyed Dad's message to the Queen. Her letter is in our family "archives."

Other letters and calls have come from transplanted southern Illinoisans across the nation who were captivated by *Foothold*. The book was reprinted in 1999 because of the continued demand. Dad did not live to see his manuscript published, but he did see a bound final draft—he read it again and again and told me, "It works me over every time." He and Mom would have enjoyed so much the many profiles of their friends and neighbors in *Growing Up in a Land Called Egypt* as well.

There is one more little story that I must share with you, dear readers. Charley informed me that Marge Miller, wife of Dr. T. O. Miller (who bought our home place from Dad in 1971), and her neighbors had decided that the name of their lane should be Caraway Road. Their petition was granted; and our family name road sign now directs travelers from Illinois Route 127 down the country lane we children walked, all our young lives, barefoot in the summer-warm dust and in brand new school shoes come fall. A recent *Southern Illinoisan* story declared that street names should be reserved for heroes. Perhaps this is the last best tribute to the author of *Foothold on a Hillside* and his beautiful wife, Bessie Mae. And it will always be a poignant reminder that we can only go home in our memories. Still, my mind turns back, again and again, to capture and follow those memories, just as the sunflowers in the backyard of the home place caught the first rays of the morning sun and followed them all the day.

> Long, long be my heart with such memories fill'd!
> Like the vase in which roses have once been distill'd:
> You may break, you may shatter the vase if you will,
> But the scent of the roses will hang round it still.
>
> —Thomas Moore, *Farewell! But Whenever . . .*

Caraway Road, just off Illinois Route 127, south of Murphysboro.

Acknowledgments

First and foremost, my special thanks must go to Arthur (Lain) Adkins, director of the Southern Illinois University Press, who recognized my book manuscript as a worthy project, and to Karl Kageff, editor in chief, who guided *Growing Up in a Land Called Egypt: A Southern Illinois Family Biography* through the publishing process with consummate skill. My appreciation extends to all others at the Press who helped shape my manuscript into a published work.

Many of the photographs featured in this book belong to me or members of my family. Others belong to area friends and neighbors who are genuinely interested in their heritage and wanted to contribute to the book.

The photographs of Fred and Lena Doody, the Doody home, Sharon School, and the Charles Ross home were contributed by Ashton Doody of Murphysboro, Illinois. He and Lillian Ross Borgmiller, also of Murphysboro, furnished some of the caption detail.

The composite photograph of the young Miltons was furnished by Lester and Maxine Hawk Milton of Murphysboro. They and Mary Milton Myers of Alto Pass, Illinois, furnished some of the caption information.

The photograph of Robert and Laura Mileur Moore and some of the caption detail were furnished by Roberta Moore Parmley of Murphysboro.

The picture of the Doy Sherwood family and some of the caption detail were contributed by Verda Sherwood Lambert of Murphysboro.

The caption detail for the photograph of Claudia Bodkin and her baby was furnished by James Oscar and Dorothy Rawson Bodkin of Carbondale, Illinois.

The picture of the Mount Pleasant Young People's Group at Little Grand Canyon and some of the caption information were furnished by Daisy Allen Lirely of Murphysboro. Geraldine Ewell and other staff of the Shawnee National Forest at Harrisburg, Illinois, also contributed caption detail.

The photograph of the Murphysboro Township High School is from the postcard collection of Ellen Brown Gates of Carbondale. Woodson Fishback's *A History of Murphysboro, Illinois, 1843–1982*, is the source of caption detail.

The photographs of Michael and Belle Kelley, the Kelley family, and June Knupp were furnished by June Knupp Bowen of Jonesboro, Illinois.

Genealogist Delores Reed Fozzard of Carterville, Illinois, and Earlene Douglass Sanders of Murphysboro contributed some of the interesting data for the chapter on African Americans in southern Illinois. And the Jackson County Historical Society of Murphysboro furnished the cemetery map presented and described in this chapter.

Helen Brewer Haney of Carbondale contributed the photographs of Martha and George Haney. She and Carvel F. Etherton of Murphysboro contributed caption information.

The photographs of Cyrus Reeves and Siota Hagler before their wedding and at their fifty-fifth anniversary celebration were furnished, with caption detail, by Anna Mae Reeves Naegele of Murphysboro.

Carldene Etherton McGhee of Murphysboro furnished the photographs of the Etherton family and their fiftieth wedding anniversary celebration and contributed some of the caption detail.

The photographs of Merritt Caraway and Melvina Powell were copied from 1878 tintypes furnished by Ethel Hiller Parrish of Carbondale and Joanne Parrish Cross of Murphysboro. Joanne also lent valued assistance in many other ways.

The photograph of William Trobaugh in his general store on the Southern Illinois University campus was contributed by Robert W. Stokes, university photographer emeritus, Carbondale. Some of the information for the caption was taken from *Daily Egyptian* and *Southern Illinoisan* articles furnished by Ann Trobaugh Gher of Champaign, Illinois.

Fannie Lirely Oliver of Makanda, Illinois, furnished the photographs of Ida Mae Elliott and the Lirely family, along with caption details.

The photograph of Logan and Ada Ellis was contributed by Barbara Ellis Davis of Makanda. Caption information was furnished by Charles Edward Ellis Sr. of Murphysboro.

The photograph of J. C. Penney Company's Murphysboro store is from the personal collection of P. Michael Jones of Murphysboro. Caption information was furnished by Richard M. Corkery, former manager of Penney's store in Carbondale.

The photograph of Ross's store in Murphysboro is from the postcard collection of Ellen Gates. Esther Ross Appleton of Boca Raton, Florida, furnished the caption information.

The photograph of the Square Deal Clothing House in Murphysboro was furnished by Burke Yeager of Murphysboro. Caption information was taken from *Daily Independent* stories furnished by the Jackson County Historical Society. Phyllis Yeager Grob and Carolyn Gallegly of Murphysboro also furnished caption information.

The photograph of the Frank Mileur family and some of the caption material was contributed by Billie Mileur Koenig. She and Carvel F. Etherton furnished portions of the caption material.

The photograph of Bessie Mae Caraway as a young matron was furnished by Betty Allen Stanley of Makanda who found the postcard picture among the personal effects of Pearl Rowan Allen, her deceased mother.

Michael J. McNerney, then president of American Resources Group, Ltd., Carbondale, identified and photographed the Indian artifacts from my home place and furnished the information used in the captions.

The photograph of William and Elzora Morefield and caption details were contributed by Esther Morefield Harris of Murphysboro.

Thelma Caraway Landrum of Columbus, Georgia, furnished the screen print of the 1846 tintype wedding photograph of William P. and Mary Jane Clemmons Caraway of Wilson County, Tennessee.

Bill Dallas of Murphysboro contributed the 1899 photograph of the William F. Caraway family of Eldorado, Illinois.

The photograph of the Mount Pleasant Methodist Church was furnished by the Reverend Paul H. Prater, then the pastor of the church. Most of the information in the caption was compiled from a videotape presentation by Linda C. Brandon for a Multi-Image Class at SIUC. Her original sources were Aaron Lloyd and Mary Alice Blessing, Daisy Lirely, and Helen Jenkins, all of Murphysboro, and Harold Cox of Carbondale. Anne Heininger Davis of Murphysboro also contributed to the caption.

Dorothy Deason Canning of Murphysboro furnished the photograph of the Ellery Deason family. She and Russell Deason of Hot Springs Village, Arkansas, contributed caption details.

The photograph of the reenactment of the 1866 Decoration Day at Hiller Cemetery was copied from a 1966 *Daily Egyptian* article. Caption information for this scene and for the photograph of Crab Orchard Christian Church was furnished by Kenneth and Virginia Baggett Lingle of Carbondale, whose sources were John W. Allen, author of *Legends & Lore of Southern Illinois*, and church documents.

The aerial photograph of the Southern Illinois Normal University campus was contributed by Robert Stokes. The caption includes historical data from promotional material prepared by the university. John Robert Odaniell, executive director emeritus, Alumni Association, SIUC, also contributed to the caption.

The photograph of Mae Allen and her daughter was furnished by George Marvin of Effingham, Illinois. Mae of Williamsburg, Virginia, and Charles Marvin of Carbondale furnished caption information.

The exceptional skills of John A. Vercillo, then scientific photographer III in the School of Medicine, SIUC, and Robert R. Morefield, chairman of photo collections for the Jackson County Historical Society, enabled me to present many historical photographs in this book. John copied with meticulous care a number of the old photographs. Bob's extensive knowledge of various area collections helped me to track down several elusive photographs that might not have surfaced otherwise. He copied many old photographs featured in this work with the dedication of a true historian.

I am also indebted to the Sallie Logan Public Library and the Jackson County Historical Society at Murphysboro, the Carbondale Public Library, SIUC's Morris Library, and the Forestry Sciences Laboratory on the SIUC campus for the excellent assistance their research specialists provided as my project came together.

Ervin Coppi, publicity promotion specialist emeritus, Broadcasting Service, SIUC, lent me his expertise on a number of occasions with his usual style and grace.

My special thanks must go to members of my immediate family—George, Ethel, Charley, Betty, and my sisters-in-law Ann and Mary—who helped me tie up many a loose thread in my fabric of remembrances. Charley also helped me locate several old photographs. And Ethel, an avid reader, called relevant bits of history to my attention.

Finally, I extend my sincere appreciation to all who participated in this project that "grew like Topsy" to enfold the lives and times of native sons and daughters in distant communities across the land.

Cleo Caraway, a native southern Illinoisan, was born and raised on a farm south of Murphysboro. A graduate of Murphysboro Township High School, she attended Southern Illinois University in Carbondale and worked for over forty years for the Forest Service, U.S. Department of Agriculture, on the SIUC campus. Caraway received the U.S. Department of Agriculture Award for Superior Service and published a history of the Forestry Sciences Laboratory on the campus of SIUC. She is the editor and compiler of her late father's book *Foothold on a Hillside: Memories of a Southern Illinoisan*, published by Southern Illinois University Press. Caraway is the author of two novels and a collection of her poems, some of which have been featured in regional magazines and newspapers.

Shawnee Books

Also available in this series . . .

The Next New Madrid Earthquake: A Survival Guide for the Midwest
WILLIAM ATKINSON

Reckoning at Eagle Creek: The Secret Legacy of Coal in the Heartland
JEFF BIGGERS

History as They Lived It: A Social History of Prairie du Rocher, Illinois
MARGARET KIMBALL BROWN

Foothold on a Hillside: Memories of a Southern Illinoisan
CHARLESS CARAWAY

Growing Up in a Land Called Egypt: A Southern Illinois Family Biography
CLEO CARAWAY

Colonial Ste. Genevieve: An Adventure on the Mississippi Frontier
CARL J. EKBERG

A Nickel's Worth of Skim Milk: A Boy's View of the Great Depression
ROBERT J. HASTINGS

A Penny's Worth of Minced Ham: Another Look at the Great Depression
ROBERT J. HASTINGS

Southern Illinois Coal: A Portfolio
C. WILLIAM HORRELL

Always of Home: A Southern Illinois Childhood
EDGAR ALLEN IMHOFF

Lives of Fort de Chartres: Commandants, Soldiers, and Civilians in French Illinois, 1720–1770
DAVID MACDONALD

Kaskaskia: The Lost Capital of Illinois
DAVID MACDONALD AND RAINE WATERS

20 Day Trips in and around the Shawnee National Forest
LARRY P. AND DONNA J. MAHAN

Land of Big Rivers: French and Indian Illinois, 1699–1778
M. J. MORGAN

America's Deadliest Twister: The Tri-State Tornado of 1925
GEOFF PARTLOW

Escape Betwixt Two Suns: A True Tale of the Underground Railroad in Illinois
CAROL PIRTLE

Fishing Southern Illinois
ART REID

All Anybody Ever Wanted of Me Was to Work: The Memoirs of Edith Bradley Rendleman
EDITH BRADLEY RENDLEMAN
EDITED BY JANE ADAMS

The Civilian Conservation Corps in Southern Illinois, 1933–1942
KAY RIPPELMEYER

Giant City State Park and the Civilian Conservation Corps: A History in Words and Pictures
KAY RIPPELMEYER

Fluorspar Mining: Photos from Illinois and Kentucky, 1905–1995
HERBERT K. RUSSELL

A Southern Illinois Album: Farm Security Administration Photographs, 1936–1943
HERBERT K. RUSSELL

The State of Southern Illinois: An Illustrated History
HERBERT K. RUSSELL